UTOPIAN WITCH

SOLARPUNK MAGICK TO FIGHT CLIMATE CHANGE AND SAVE THE WORLD

JUSTINE NORTON-KERTSON

Microcosm Publishing
Portland, Ore | Cleveland, Ohio

UTOPIAN WITCH: SOLARPUNK MAGICK TO FIGHT CLIMATE CHANGE AND SAVE THE WORLD

© Justine Norton-Kertson, 2024
© This edition Microcosm Publishing 2024
First edition - 3,000 copies - July 23, 2024
ISBN 9781648412523
This is Microcosm #799
Cover by Lindsey Cleworth
Edited by Kandi Zeller
Illustrated by Aspen Muskovich and the author
Design by Joe Biel

To join the ranks of high-class stores that feature Microcosm titles, talk to your rep: In the U.S. COMO (Atlantic), ABRAHAM (Midwest), BOB BARNETT (Texas, Oklahoma, Arkansas, Louisiana), IMPRINT (Pacific), TURNAROUND (UK), UTP/MANDA (Canada), NEWSOUTH (Australia/New Zealand), Observatoire (Africa, Europe), IPR (Middle East), Yvonne Chau (Southeast Asia), HarperCollins (India), Everest/B.K. Agency (China), Tim Burland (Japan/Korea), and FAIRE and EMERALD in the gift trade.

For a catalog, write or visit:
Microcosm Publishing
2752 N Williams Ave.
Portland, OR 97227

All the news that's fit to print at www.Microcosm.Pub/Newsletter.

Get more copies of this book at www.Microcosm.Pub/UtopianWitch.

For more witchy books, visit www.Microcosm.Pub/Witchy.

Did you know that you can buy our books directly from us at sliding scale rates? Support a small, independent publisher and pay less than Amazon's price at **www. Microcosm.Pub.**

Global labor conditions are bad, and our roots in industrial Cleveland in the '70s and '80s made us appreciate the need to treat workers right. Therefore, our books are MADE IN THE USA.

Library of Congress Cataloging-in-Publication Data 2023050629

MICROCOSM · PUBLISHING

MICROCOSM PUBLISHING is Portland's most diversified publishing house and distributor, with a focus on the colorful, authentic, and empowering. Our books and zines have put your power in your hands since 1996, equipping readers to make positive changes in their lives and in the world around them. Microcosm emphasizes skill-building, showing hidden histories, and fostering creativity through challenging conventional publishing wisdom with books and bookettes about DIY skills, food, bicycling, gender, self-care, and social justice. What was once a distro and record label started by Joe Biel in a drafty bedroom was determined to be *Publishers Weekly*'s fastest-growing publisher of 2022 and #3 in 2023 and 2024, and is now among the oldest independent publishing houses in Portland, OR, and Cleveland, OH. We are a politically moderate, centrist publisher in a world that has inched to the right for the past 80 years.

CONTENTS

Introduction

WHAT IS SOLARPUNK?

*T*had professors who used to insist that they, in their role as teachers, were activists. They were right, but I don't believe teachers automatically fit this term just by virtue of their day job. The way those particular professors approached their role and the teaching methods they used turned their teaching into activism, i.e. something that disrupts the status quo with the goal of creating social and political change.

The same is true of literature and other kinds of art. Telling a story or creating a work of visual art can be an exercise in activism, depending on the message you're trying to convey and why. A coming of age story might not inherently be a work of activism. On the other hand, a coming of age story about BIPOC or queer youth navigating and challenging racist, heteronormative institutions, by design, starts conversations that will hopefully lead to real world change.

Solarpunk is a wonderful example of speculative fiction[1] that brings art and real-world activism together in a shared purpose—to create a better world. It's still a relatively new subgenre of science fiction, and there's plenty of disagreement about what qualifies as solarpunk.[2] But there does seem to be general agreement that we can use this genre as a foundation for understanding and exploration.

Solarpunk stories are about futures where humanity seeks to live in harmony with nature. They're tales where we've either solved or are in the process of working together to creatively and optimistically adapt to climate change. Stories in the genre are about social justice and equality, Indigenous sovereignty and leadership, antiauthoritarianism, and ending the system of capitalist, western, white, cis-male-hetero supremacy.

Those themes and a hopeful, utopian tone are the backdrop against which solarpunk stories exist and are told. This is activist art. It's imagining a new and better world that's rooted in communities tackling social problems and global challenges. It proposes solutions and shows people enacting them. Rather than ending with apocalypse and dystopia, solarpunk uses apocalypse and the collapse of dystopia as a starting place. From there, it weaves tales proposing creative—even if fictional—solutions to rebuilding society.

This rebuilding idea is where the *punk* in solarpunk comes in. The term *punk* is loaded with connotations and stereotypes. Some of these include spiked hair, clothing with holes and safety pins (and other metal spikes), body piercings, loud and angry

---

1 According to Dictionary.com, *speculative fiction* is an umbrella term for genres that include elements of science fiction, fantasy, horror, or the supernatural.

2 One of the more common points of dispute I've seen in various solarpunk forums online is between two groups. The first group looks enthusiastically, and even sometimes uncritically, to technology to help solve global problems. On the other hand, those in the second group are either a) primitivists who generally eschew technology or b) people who are accepting of new technological solutions, but only after a lot of scrutiny.

music, disrespect for authority and social norms, drug use, and houseless kids with banjos, ukuleles, and mandolins strapped to their backs out busking on street corners. While *-punk* subgenres of literature are born out of that same general punk movement that began in 1970s Britain, they've also now grown into their own unique phenomenon.

Like the larger punk movement, punk speculative fiction genres center on the value of rebellion. The two most well known punk genres illustrate this point well. You'll be hard pressed to find a cyberpunk story out there in which the protagonist and their crew aren't rebelling and fighting against a corrupt corporation (or corporate government) that uses technology as a means of control and oppression.

Steampunk stories too have, at their heart, the theme of rebellion against the powerful and corrupt. Ecopunk narratives are also all about rebelling against a corrupt and broken system: a rebellion against fossil fuel companies and a system entrenched in a mode of energy production that is damaging our planet and civilization.

Enter solarpunk, one of the newest punk literary genres.

The term *solarpunk* was coined in a 2008 article published on the blog *Republic of Bees*.[3] The article suggested a new literary genre grounded in futures with renewable energy and resource based economies. That article also laid out a very basic framework for the new literary genre by comparing it to steampunk, which at the time was enjoying its own moment in the sun.

Interestingly, while it is often claimed—and not without justifiable reasoning—that solarpunk sprung up as a reaction to cyberpunk, the author of the article that coined the term and first introduced the genre to the world told a different story. In

---

3 "From Steampunk to Solarpunk," *Republic of Bees*, May 27, 2008, republicofthebees. wordpress.com/2008/05/27/from-steampunk-to-solarpunk/.

the article, "From Steampunk to Solarpunk," they quite clearly state that the idea for solarpunk was, in fact, as the article's title suggests, derived from steampunk. Indeed, both solarpunk and steampunk tell stories rooted in the conflation of modern and older technologies. Steampunk blends Victorian-era technologies with modern tech as a workaround for electricity, which wasn't widely available until the twentieth century. For solarpunk, it's about bringing older technologies such as wind power into the modern era, in order to eliminate the use of fossil fuels and mitigate the damage such use has already caused.

But when it comes to envisioning future solutions, solarpunk isn't just about flashy new tech, it's about people too, and it's common for solarpunk fiction and art to envision communities where BIPOC and LGBTQIA+ people are at the forefront. In these stories, folks from marginalized populations create futures that are as genuinely diverse as reality, and are led by the communities that have been colonized and oppressed in the nonfictional present and past.[4] In this way, solarpunk not only uses art and literature to propose solutions to the climate crisis, but it also joins other subgenres such as afrofuturism and amazofuturism in using art and literature to consciously and purposefully challenge global systems of oppression.

Solarpunk isn't confined to the realms of art and literature though. Nor is it confined to the proposed futures of speculative storytelling. Solarpunks are out in the present world right now, working to build the better future we envision. Around the world in both virtual and physical spaces, solarpunks work together to prefigure the world we want to create by living sustainably and building networks of radically optimistic communities. One example of this is @TheSolarpunkFarmer on YouTube and other

---

4 For more on this idea of solarpunk as anti-imperialist, Rob Cameron's article "In Search of Afro-Solarpunk, Part 1: Elements of Afrofuturism" is a good place to start and has a decent list of sources at the end: tor.com/2019/10/29/in-search-of-afro-solarpunk-part-1-elements-of-afrofuturism/.

social media,who shares knowledge about how to build a better world through sustainable gardening, permaculture, and local food production.

Solarpunks continue to join on the frontlines of struggles against pipelines, fossil fuels, deforestation, and other projects that would seriously damage the land, water, and air. Additionally, solarpunks are at the forefront of the struggle for animal rights, and we're helping develop climate solutions of all kinds.The list could easily go on.

In summary, solarpunk is literature, art, fashion, cuisine, music, and architecture. It's also activism and community-building, problem-solving through prefigurative praxis[5], and using radical hope as fuel for creative disruption in service of a better future. This unique combination gives solarpunk the power to change the world.

MAGICKAL ETHICS

In this journey of spirituality and magick, it's vital to take a moment for a discussion about ethics. Our practice, just like our lives, doesn't exist in a vacuum where consequences don't exist. It interacts with the world around us, influencing as well as being influenced. This is especially true when we engage with magick in a political context. While we strive for change and justice, it is essential to remember the core tenets of our Craft.

While I'm an anarchist at heart, who believes in the value of a diversity of tactics, I wish to make it clear: while it's up to each individual to decide where to draw their own ethical lines, this book does not advocate for using magick to endanger or physically

---

5 A quick note about this term, which isn't very common outside of leftist activist circles. *Prefigure* means "to show," and *praxis* means "action or practice." So prefigurative praxis is basically practicing what you preach. Rather than waiting for slow, incremental changes that may not come, you become a living example by building the world you want right now in whatever ways you can, right here in the middle of all the current mess.

harm anyone, regardless of their actions or beliefs. This holds true even when doing spells related to those who actively cause harm through oppressive systems, fascism, fossil fuel extraction, and other damaging activities. We might vehemently disagree with them, organize against their actions, and work tirelessly for change, but causing physical harm goes against basic Craft principles.

Why, you might ask? Because every person has their own journey, and who are we to dictate the course of their life? Second, because most witches and magickal practitioners believe our magick is bound by the Law of Threefold Return, also known as the Rule of Three. This rule states that whatever energy or magick a witch puts out into the world, regardless of whether the intention is positive or negative, will return to them threefold. If we channel harmful energy, we are inviting that same energy back into our lives. This is not to say that we can't protect ourselves, but rather, that any protection should be about creating shields and barriers, not about actively and purposefully causing injury and trauma to others.

Instead of focusing on causing harm, I encourage you to utilize magick as a tool for hopeful and positive change. We can use our energy to heal, to protect, to enlighten, and to fight for justice in ways that aren't designed to physically harm others. We can work magick that aims to expose the truth, encourages people to see the harmful effects of their actions, and opens hearts and minds to more compassionate perspectives.

We can also use magick to bolster our mundane actions. Protesting, organizing, educating others, supporting local and sustainable businesses that treat their employees well and pay a living wage, providing mutual aid—these are all incredibly powerful actions that can foster immense change, and our magick can lend them even more potency.

Our Craft is rooted in respect—for ourselves, for others, and for the Earth. As witches, we're intimately connected to the rhythms of the natural world, and we understand that all life is deeply and meaningfully interconnected. It's our charge and our responsibility, both as witches and as compassionate human beings, to approach our Craft—and our lives—with mindfulness, compassion, and respect for the intrinsic value of all beings.

THE URGENCY OF THE WORK

After decades of dystopian dominance in our culture through TV, movies, comic books, politics, and the twenty-four-hour news cycle, solarpunk and utopianism are making waves.[6] For those who may not be familiar with the term, a great way to describe solarpunk is that it's a movement in art, literature, architecture, fashion, and activism that attempts to answer the question of what a sustainable world looks like and how we can get there.[7]

Many are fed up with pessimism—their own and that of those around them—which so easily embraces apathy. Others are fueled by a radical hope born from the struggle to overcome lifetimes of oppression. Still others began blending their spiritual craft practice and their political activism years ago. In fact, activism motivated by spiritual conviction goes back at least centuries and more.[8] Still, now more than ever, we've simply had enough of our

---

6 Nicola K. Smith, "What Is Solarpunk and Can It Help Save the Planet?" BBC. August 3, 2021, bbc.com/news/business-57761297.

7 Juan David Reina-Rozo. "Art, Energy and Technology: the Solarpunk Movement," *International Journal of Engineering, Social Justice, and Peace*, 8 (1): 47–60. March 5, 2021, doi:10.24908/ijesjp.v8i1.14292

8 Spiritually motivated activism isn't necessarily progressive, however. The so-called Religious Right, for example, uses its influence, wealth, and political power to further the causes of restricting the rights of women and LGBTQIA+ folks. On the other hand, pacifist Quakers who refused to take up arms during the American Revolutionary War are a great example of more progressive but still spiritually motivated activism. Another well known example of progressive spiritual activism is the U.S. Civil Rights Era of the 1950s and1960s, which was heavily influenced by liberal and even radically leftist religious leaders such as the Reverend Dr. Martin Luther King Jr. and Malcolm X.

society's reactionary and regressive descent into science fiction hellscapes.

It's time to demand utopia, and that's exactly what we're doing. We're not only demanding utopia, but we're doing the work to build a better world right now. And it's happening all over the planet, including right here in the United States, the current seat of global empire.

The urgency of the task before us—to prevent the worst of the coming climate catastrophe—couldn't be more clear. It's well beyond the scope of this book to delve into climate science and socio-political class analysis of modern society. But if you're here and you're reading this book, it's safe to assume you understand the urgency of the climate crisis: rapidly melting glaciers, rising ocean levels, sinking islands, increasingly frequent and powerful hurricanes, wildfires, and other climate related natural disasters get worse by the year.

It can also be safely assumed that if you're here reading this book, then you're aware of the very real threat posed by the growth of neofascism and the extreme, insurrectionist right wing over the past decade. You no doubt believe black lives matter and want to work to upset systems of white supremacy. And you understand the threat posed by militarized police, who have for too long been treated as above the law in practice, if not in the letter, of the law.

Since you're familiar with this urgency, there isn't much to say about it within the scope of this book other than to reiterate that urgency's existence and growth with each passing day. If you aren't familiar with how urgent issues like climate change and white supremacy are, you can head to the appendix on page 249 for a list of recommended resources.

One thing that does need to be said about this urgency is that spiritual practice and performing magick alone aren't and never will be enough to solve the monumental challenges with which solarpunks are concerned and with which our world is faced. It's of the utmost importance for solarpunk witches to be on the ground in environmental and social justice struggles to the extent that each is able.

This practical, "mundane," on-the-ground work is absolutely vital. Spiritual practice and performing magick helps bring us focus and purpose in our work. It helps us connect to nature and to other humans in ways that are important for solarpunk and building utopian, resilient communities. But we also need to realize that magick rarely, if ever, is something that works like "presto change-o." Our solarpunk magick and spiritual practice should inspire us to go out and be an active part of building those communities, and of creating and implementing the solutions.

WHO AM I?

As the founder and co-editor-in-chief of *Solarpunk Magazine*,[9] I've not only had a front row seat to, but have also had the privilege of helping shepherd, the literary aspect of the solarpunk genre and movement through the explosive growth it's experienced in recent years. It's my hope that this book will help further the growth of the genre by bringing solarpunk into the realm of spirituality, bridging the small gap between solarpunk's Earth-based values and neo-pagan witchcraft, and through an infusion of leftist, radical, solarpunk politics, rescuing New Age spiritual paths from their recent and dangerous flirtations with the extremist right wing.[10]

---

9 solarpunkmagazine.com

10 The COVID-19 pandemic brought together an unlikely alliance between certain factions of the pagan, New Age communities and right-wing conspiracy theorists, both groups championing anti-vaccination sentiment and resisting precautionary measures against the virus. It's a disconcerting merger, given the stark ideological differences between the two groups. Many individuals in the pagan and New Age communities typically embrace progressive ideals, advocating for environmental protection, social justice, and inclusivity. On the other hand, extremist right-wing conspiracy theorists often propagate exclusionary, nativist, and regressive ideologies. Yet their shared

I've studied and practiced witchcraft since I was about seventeen years old, over a quarter of a century. I still remember the day a friend gave me a copy of *The Spiral Dance* by Starhawk.[11] That book changed my life. Her science fantasy novel *The Fifth Sacred Thing*,[12] which I read soon after, turned out to be my first exposure to a literary genre that would eventually be termed *solarpunk*. And her own passion for and practice of spiritual activism has not only been a long time inspiration for my own spirituality and activist work, but also for this book.

Not long after I turned nineteen, I started taking my first group classes at New Age and witchcraft shops in Southern California, where I was attending the University of California, Irvine. studying U.S. imperialism and world religions. At twenty-one, I was initiated into my first coven, which was part of an eclectic, neo-Druidic tradition. By age twenty-three, I was teaching introductory courses for our network of covens. I've practiced witchcraft ever since. My partner and I taught the Craft to our kids and had a family coven as we raised them. Currently, I'm currently an Ovate grade member of the Order of Bards, Ovates, and Druids.

My first taste of political activism came not long before I was first introduced to witchcraft. When I was sixteen years old, a couple other students and I refused to stand for the Pledge of Allegiance during high school homeroom. Sent to the vice principal's office by our math teacher (who was also a former air force officer) for disciplinary action, we asserted our court-

---

distrust of authority, emphasis on personal freedoms and sovereignty, and suspicions of mainstream medicine provided common ground. It's a testament to the confusing, distressing times we're living in, where fear and misinformation can blur boundaries and create strange bedfellows. As solarpunk witches, we should critically examine these developments, reassert the importance of fact-based information, and promote a balance between individual rights and communal wellbeing.

11 Starhawk, *The Spiral Dance: A Rebirth of the Ancient Religion of the Great Goddess, 10th Anniversary Edition* (San Francisco: HarperSan Francisco, 1997).

12 Starhawk, *The Fifth Sacred Thing*. (New York: Bantam, 1994).

established right to remain seated[13] and—other than a long and uselessly cliché lecture about patriotism and obedience—we didn't get punished.

During my college years, my political activism and organizing skills began to blossom alongside my budding new spiritual path. It's no coincidence that as I delved into Earth-based spiritual traditions, it drew me to activism work focused on the environment. I helped found a campus branch of CalPIRG, which is a network of student-led environmentalist and consumer watchdog organizations.[14] Running local campaigns related to pesticides in schools and clean water, I was elected as the organization's state board vice chair in 1999.

It was during that time I also got my first taste of labor organizing, which became a major part of my later career as a community organizer. I helped organize student worker strike[15] prep by leading undergraduate outreach for the Associated Student Employee Union's UC Irvine branch.

My activist life continued into the early 2000s with the fight to win, and then to save, same-sex marriage in California. Then, in 2011, only a couple years after moving to Oregon, I dropped out of grad school to join Occupy Portland. It was then that my leftist radicalization began in earnest. My experiences during that time were formative for my anti-capitalist perspectives and belief in the need to dismantle police forces, and this was also a foundational time for my later work organizing with houseless communities.

After my experience at Occupy Portland, I immersed myself in radical political organizing and activist work. I've been

13 West Virginia State Board of Education v. Barnette, 319 U.S. 624 (1943). In this case, the U.S. Supreme Court ruled that public school students can't be forced to salute, or stand and recite, the pledge allegiance to the U.S. flag.
14 calpirgstudents.org
15 Kenneth R. Weiss, "UC Teaching Assistants Strike on 8 Campuses." *Los Angeles Times,* December 2, 1998, latimes.com/archives/la-xpm-1998-dec-02-mn-49849-story.html.

arrested numerous times during business shutdowns, public space occupations, and workplace strike actions. I've engaged in eviction defense, advocated for a Houseless Bill of Rights and engaged in houseless camp eviction defense as well as antifascist and radical labor work.

In 2014, I planned and hosted the first 15 Now PDX meeting and became the campaign manager for Oregon's $15 minimum wage ballot measure, which successfully won a $15 minimum wage for some 26 Oregon cities, and other raises for the rest of the state.[16] I also facilitated community defense trainings.

Through the work I did on minimum wage issues, I became heavily involved with Don't Shoot Portland and had the privilege of working closely with its founder, Teresa Raiford, in a variety of capacities over the years. In 2015, at an early Don't Shoot Portland rally, I had the honor of sharing a stage with the Reverend Jesse Jackson on the steps of Portland (in)Justice Center,[17] where I spoke about the relationship between racial justice and raising the minimum wage.

Despite my eventual focus on class politics and labor organizing, I've never strayed from my environmentalist roots. One reason for this? Human-induced climate change is intimately related to our economic activity and its foundation in extractive fossil fuel usage. All justice issues—climate change, class, race, and capitalist greed, power, patriarchy, and imperialism, to name just a few—intersect and mingle with each other. The same is true in my own life. My witchcraft practice and political activism began at the same time. They each influenced the other and brought me to this place and time—to this book.

---

16 Alejandro Lazo, "Oregon Governor Signs Landmark Minimum-Wage Law." *The Wall Street Journal*, March 2, 2016. wsj.com/articles/oregon-governor-poised-to-sign-landmark-minimum-wage-bill-into-law-1456933247.

17 Bryan Denson. "Jesse Jackson, at Portland Protest, Says Ferguson Policeman Darren Wilson's Resignation 'a Step in the Right Direction'." *Oregon Live*, November 30, 2014, oregonlive.com/portland/2014/11/jesse_jackson_at_portland_prot.html.

It's a joy for me to bring together my witchcraft practice and activism under the banner of my current work within the solarpunk movement. And so here we are, together, sitting with this book, about to engage in a new generation of spiritual activist work together, in full knowledge that we move forward upon the shoulders of our ancestors and those who've come before in this world and in this work.

WHO IS THIS BOOK FOR?

This book is for you!

Of all the books you could have opened and taken a browse at, you chose this one. And perhaps, it also chose you. Either way, something drew you here. And somewhere in these pages, you're likely to find what you're looking for, or at least the trailhead to the path that will get you there.

Whether you're a novice who is just beginning to explore magick and Earth-based spirituality, or a seasoned witch searching for new ways of using magick to support your political activism, fight climate change, and work toward utopia—you're not only going to find this book useful, but hopefully, you'll find yourself picking it up again and again, referencing the pages, words, and ideas herein.

Throughout this book, you'll find tables, appendices, charts, scripts, and graphics full of valuable information, such as magickal correspondences and symbols, sigils, and outlines for Sabbats, Esbats, and other rituals. Additionally, you'll find deep dives on nature spirituality and its relationship to solarpunk, plus spells, charms, and other magickal workings to enrich your political activism and community building.

In the echoing halls of our collective wisdom, each footstep we take towards understanding magick and Earth-based spirituality—and in our pursuit of activism and change—

contributes to the larger journey we're all on. This book serves not just as a guide, but also as a lighthouse in the mystical fog that invites both beginners and experienced practitioners alike. In your hands is a tool, a mentor, and a companion, unlocking doors to untapped realms of thought, practice, and perspective.

The journey towards utopia, towards a greener world, begins with a single step. You've taken yours by choosing this book; now, let it guide you, inspire you, and serve as your trusted partner. Every time you come back to its pages, may you find not only reference and wisdom, but also a reminder of your strength, determination, and the transformative magick that already exists within you. This is not just a book—it is an invitation to exploration, an initiation into your personal and communal empowerment.

Embrace the journey, and remember, this book truly is for you.

WHAT YOU'LL FIND IN THIS BOOK

In Part One of this solarpunk book of shadows, we'll explore some basics to give us a solid and shared foundation for the rest of the book. In Chapter One, we discuss the basics of both solarpunk and witchcraft as well their commonalities and points of intersection. In Chapter Two, we dive into the ideas of radical hope, radical politics, and how those can intersect with our magickal practice as solarpunk witches. Then, in Chapter Three, we talk about the Sun and the Earth as planets, deities, archetypes, and energies, and their importance within the framework of solarpunk witchcraft.

Part Two begins by outline a basic ritual for solarpunk witches in Chapter Four. Then, in Chapter Five, we learn about pagan celebrations, such as Sabbats and Esbats, and how we can celebrate those occasions as solarpunk witches specifically. In Chapter Six, we dive head first into Sun Magick, including meditations, correspondences, and spellwork. We wrap up Part Two with

Chapter Seven, which follows the same outline as Chapter Six, but for the Earth instead of the Sun.

The third and final section of this book completes our solarpunk book of shadows with a series of solarpunk spells rooted in environmental and social justice, and working toward our shared vision of a more compassionate, healthy, harmonious, and utopian world.

I recognize that this may seem western-centric, and I recognize that and its inherent limitations. However, not only is comparative political analysis outside the scope of this book, but that is the political spectrum and reality in which I live and with which I'm most directly and intimately familiar. It makes the most sense for me to write from that perspective. That isn't meant in any way to negate the relevance and importance of different political realities and perspectives throughout the rest of the world. If that's a topic you want to delve into, a list of resources is provided in the "Social Justice Resources" section of the appendix at the back of the book that can get you started on that exploration.

Chapter Eight contains spells for fighting and adapting to climate change, including protection spells for extreme weather events, spells to take on fossil fuel companies, and more. Chapter Nine is full of spellwork for other environmental issues that aren't necessarily or directly related to climate change, such as protecting clean air, soil, and water, stopping deforestation, and protecting endangered species from extinction. The tenth chapter of the book presents spells to use around other important, global social issues, such as the rise of fascism and supremacism, borders and anti-immigrant hysteria, and ending capitalism and imperialism. Finally, in Chapter Eleven, I provide guidelines for creating your own solarpunk spells. In addition, you can find lists of various additional resources at the end of the book in the appendix.

THE NECESSITY OF DOING THE MATERIAL WORK

It's important for me to say a few words up front about doing magickal work for political issues of great consequence, such as those solarpunks concern themselves with. We're talking about changing the world. We're talking about serious socio-political issues that are deeply relevant and impactful for people's material lives and welfare.

Since solarpunk's inception, its utopian futures have contained a variety of social justice assumptions. As already stated, a world that has moved beyond the exploitative greed of capitalism is one of the premises on which solarpunk is founded. Post-scarcity economics (i.e. ensuring everyone has enough not only to survive, but to thrive) and antiauthoritarianism are also strong solarpunk values. As such, it should come as no surprise that a significant segment of the solarpunk community leans toward either socialism, anarchism, or some kind of mixture of the two, such as syndicalism or anarcho-socialism.

Other socio-political assumptions include a system based on cooperation rather than competition, as well as a world freed from white supremacy, patriarchy, corporate-political corruption, western imperialism, and settler colonialism. Further, and central to the genre, utopian solarpunk futures exist in a world where humanity has used a combination of technology and social changes to adapt to and ultimately resolve the climate crisis. As such, humanity in solarpunk futures lives in harmony and cooperation with nature and technology.

Therefore, a number of things are decidedly not solarpunk when it comes to politics. Here and there, people in various forums have tried—in one way or another—to claim these ideas as potential characteristics of solarpunk, or as things that could coexist with it. But for reasons I detail below, these ideas typically receive vociferous backlash from within the solarpunk community.

As already mentioned, capitalism is decidedly not solarpunk, and yet it isn't uncommon for people within the community to push some kind of modified capitalism with an eco-friendly facade. There have been, and no doubt will continue to be, those who believe achieving a more just and utopian future is possible through or with the help of some form of capitalism. I am decidedly not one of them, but such people are out there. I firmly believe, as do most solarpunks, that utopianism isn't compatible with exploitation, greed, and profit-based economics, all of which are foundational to capitalism.

Similar to, or perhaps even a part of, capitalism is the concept of greenwashing.[18] The term doesn't refer to environmentally friendly soaps and laundry detergents, or maybe it does. But if so, it's more about the way those products are marketed than the products themselves, and greenwashing is by no means limited to products that have some kind of real, even if relative, environmental benefit.

Greenwashing is a kind of marketing that exploits people's desire to do the right thing and be part of the solution, even if only in a small way. The end goal of greenwashers isn't to stop climate change and build a better world, however. Rather, its aim is to generate profit for companies and shareholders by convincing people, whom they insultingly refer to as "consumers," that products are more environmentally friendly and better for the planet than they actually are.

A good example of greenwashing is branding electric vehicles as eco-friendly. One day they might be. It would even be fair to say we're closer to that branding being accurate than we were a quarter century ago when the first hybrid and fully electric vehicles hit the market. Still, even to this day, almost two-thirds of the electricity we use in the U.S. is produced by burning fossil fuels, including

---

18 Greenwashing refers to the practice of using marketing spin to fool people into believing products or ideas are environmentally friendly when they actually aren't. The term "clean coal" is a good example of greenwashing.

coal,[19] which is even worse than oil is for the environment and for the prognosis regarding climate change.[20]

Ecofascism is another contrary-to-solarpunk idea which manages to rear its ugly head all too often. While I've never seen anyone use or advocate for the term *ecofascism* itself, it's not uncommon in solarpunk forums to see people make comments that are at best, poorly thought out and extremely conspicuous. Blaming overpopulation for climate change is one of these slippery slopes; it's often associated with eugenics, for example, and ends in genocide if followed through to its logical conclusion.

There's also a strain within a strain of anarchism that falls into this category of things that are contrary to, but make recurring appearances in, present-day solarpunk spaces. Anarcho-primitivism is a subset of eco-anarchism that insists collapse is not only inevitable, but desired. It claims that technology is incapable of solving the problem of climate change or existing in a harmonious relationship with humanity and nature. This socio-political philosophy asserts that if we're ever going to live in harmony with nature, we must significantly reduce and severely restrict our use of technology, even if it isn't based on fossil fuel use.

While there may be a certain romanticism to the notion of human civilization returning to a more primitive state, upon closer inspection it suffers from the same problems as ecofascism, and indeed is perhaps even a gateway to the latter. A reduction in electricity use and technology to the extent suggested by primitivism results in genocide. How many people living with disabilities won't last very long without benefits of electricity and modern technology? How many essential medications will go unmade because we need the

19 According to the U.S. Energy Information Administration, among fossil fuels, coal alone accounts for about 20 percent of U.S. electricity production, which is as much as we produce using renewable resources like solar and wind combined, and more than we produce using nuclear power: eia.gov/tools/faqs/faq.php?id=427&t=3

20 Hannah Ritchie,"What Are the Safest and Cleanest Sources of Energy?", Our World in Data, February 10, 2020, ourworldindata.org/safest-sources-of-energy#:~:text=Coal%2C%20again%2C%20is%20the%20dirtiest,a%20lesser%20extent%20than%20coal.

energy or technological capacity to produce them? How will people who use wheelchairs navigate public space when sidewalks and other concrete pathways deteriorate and crumble? Will this cost be worth it just to fulfill some notion that is at best naive, and at worse racism akin to the stereotype of the noble savage?[21]

When it comes to critical justice issues, it isn't enough to do magick and then go about our days as if all is right in the world. All is not right, and we need all hands on deck. That means we can't leave meaningful issues and needed changes to blind faith, prayer, or magick alone. No amount of desire and intention, no matter how focused, is going to change the world's horrors into flower bouquets and sunny days.

In order to create a better world, we also have to put in necessary work in the physical world to manifest our magick and our prayers. It can't be overstated how important it is that we take concrete action to make our desires for social and environmental justice real in the world. This is true of any magick we do with any goal in mind, of course. But it bears special emphasis here, given the solarpunk ethos and the nature of the discussion and spellwork we'll engage in throughout this book.

With that in mind, the justice oriented spells in Part Three are followed by lists of practical and concrete steps and actions you

---

21 "Noble savage" is a term dating back to the sixteenth century and the so-called Age of Exploration, which refers to a widespread myth that in various forms is still all too common among the New Age community today. According to the myth, early primitive humans lived in a golden age of harmony and virtue, and Indigenous, tribal people encountered by European explorers and immigrants were living models of that ideal. Four hundred years ago, this idea was considered progressive compared to the common counter notion of the so-called "brutal savage" the idea that Indigenous peoples were subhuman "animals" who needed to be converted, enslaved, or exterminated to make room for "progress." But in fact, the idea of the noble savage—both then and now—ignores the reality of violence in ancient human societies while at the same time dehumanizes modern Indigenous people by turning them into mythical stereotypes who must remain trapped in a past that never actually existed in order to maintain their assigned virtue. Back in 2001, *The Guardian* published an article titled, "Racists created the Noble Savage," that serves as a great starting point for learning more about the noble savage trope's racist roots: theguardian.com/world/2001/apr/15/socialsciences.highereducation.

can take on your own or with a group to bolster and reinforce your spellwork in the material world.

A NOTE ON THE USE OF LANGUAGE

Before we begin, I want to include a few words about the way I use language in this book. First, I'll address common terms and phrases used by religions and believers in general, as well as within the Craft and New Age, pagan spirituality specifically.

When I first moved away from my hometown and started taking group classes about the Craft, I was also taking my first classes about the history and philosophy of skepticism in general, and atheism in particular. I'm one of a growing number of atheopagans: people who have a deep respect for and spiritual practice centered on nature and the Earth, but don't believe in gods. This doesn't mean I don't use deities in my magickal work and spiritual practice. I do, but for me, they're archetypes that I can study, connect with, get to know, and learn from rather than being entities that I believe I can communicate or curry favor with in any meaningful sense outside of my own mind, imagination, and life.

This doesn't mean I think theists are wrong. Personally, I see no good reason to believe in gods. But I recognize the value they hold for many people in this world. I recognize the important contributions religious communities have played in struggles for social justice. And I recognize that while science is the best tool we have for investigating and discovering the nature of the universe, we are far from having it all figured out. There's so much we don't understand about the nature of existence. So while I'm not a believer myself, I'm also not arrogant enough to assume I know the answer.

I bring this up here not to disparage believers and their faith, but rather to be open and honest with readers about who I am, my experience, where I come from, and the perspective from which my spirituality and this book come. I still use spiritual and New Age language throughout the book, but I don't use it as heavily as perhaps other Craft authors do. And when I use words like *soul*, for example, I use them metaphorically. You should read such words in whatever way and from whatever perspective works best for you and your own path.

I also use inclusive language throughout the book. Wherever appropriate, I use gender neutral pronouns. For example, when referring to archetypes of Sun deities in the third person, I use gender neutral pronouns because Sun deities around the world and throughout time have been assigned different genders. As a trans, genderfluid person myself, I feel it makes the most sense to use gender neutral pronouns in such situations.

I also make a conscious effort throughout the book to use inclusive language in other ways. For example, you'll notice that instead of saying *stand* I'll often say *sit*, or a combination of the two, "sit or stand." Where generally in our language we would use the word *walk*, I use *move* or other similar alternatives instead. I note this because it's important to the solarpunk ethos. Solarpunk isn't just about solutions to climate change, but also to other social problems such as bigotry, imperialism, alienation, and isolation. There are a myriad of problems that need to be solved in order to create utopia on Earth. Using inclusive language is one small but important way we can help shift our culture and society in the direction of inclusiveness and empathy. That's the solarpunk way.

Part One:

Understanding Solarpunk Witchcraft

*S*triving for harmony and balance between ourselves and our tech-based civilization on the one hand, and nature the other; a deep respect for the Earth, its systems, and its cycles; the recognition of animal sentience and right to a healthy life; the desire and readiness to build a better future for those who come into and live in this world after us. This list isn't exhaustive, but it serves to illustrate the numerous points of commonality and intersection that exist between solarpunk and the Craft.

There are important differences as well. Chief among them is that in the work to build utopia, solarpunk is concerned with concrete, real world, scientific, and technological solutions to global problems like climate change. And while it's certainly emphasized within the Craft that you have to put out effort in the physical world to manifest your spellwork, the focus is still on the fantastic, on magickal and spiritual solutions more than it is on practical solutions, organizing, or activist work.

That said, the similarities abound, and from my perspective as a solarpunk and a witch, the two fit together in a unique and special way that can revolutionize the world and the way we interact with it and each other. This first section then takes us through some of the important basics of this special relationship. Its purpose is to give us a shared foundation from which we can move forward together through the rest of the book. We'll also discuss the power of radical hope and how it can aid us in our magickal activism. Then, we'll go over the power of the Sun and Earth to solarpunk witchcraft as a whole.

Chapter One: Solarpunk and Witchcraft—A Natural Relationship

Solarpunk is a movement that not only asks but tries to provide answers to the question: "What would a sustainable civilization look like and how can we get there?"[22] The answers to that question come in the form of science fiction, as well as art, activism, and fashion, which have been solarpunk's central arenas of expression. There's also an increasing recognition within the solarpunk community that balancing and restoring humanity's relationship with nature means a need for a solarpunk spirituality. Because witchcraft shares so many solarpunk values, it is a wonderful fit to satisfy this need.

To begin, let's take a closer look at the above central question of solarpunk before we delve into magick and spellwork. There's a ton of nuance we can pull from that question or definition, and I've yet to see another definition that doesn't say essentially the same thing, even if the focus is slightly different.

Solarpunk began as a literary and art movement as well as a political, social justice movement. It places considerable emphasis on the transformation of society from its current state into one that is socially, culturally, economically, and environmentally sustainable. Simply put, solarpunk is firmly grounded in utopianism and is decidedly not dystopian.

At the same time, even while solarpunk is utopian to the core, as a politically and activist driven literary genre, it's also much more concerned with possible futures than it is with alternative or fanciful futures. So solarpunk isn't just the story of what the world is like once a sustainable utopia is in place. It's also the story of how we get from here to there, how we effectively move from our

---

22 The question in this form was first posed by Jay Springett, who was one of the first solarpunk thinkers and theorists: medium.com/solarpunks/solarpunk-a-reference-guide-8bcf18871965

current state of dystopia to that better and more just world we're all striving for. It's about imagining what a sustainable world looks like.

As a genre, solarpunk embraces technology as an important part of the solution to prevent climate change. Specifically, it emphasizes the development of a harmonious relationship between humanity, technology, and nature. The extent to which this relationship is currently out of balance can be seen when solarpunk is juxtaposed to other -punk literary genres. In the cyberpunk science fiction genre, for example, powerful and corrupt corporate politicians often use advanced and futuristic technology as a weapon against both nature and their fellow humans. In such stories, the relationship between humanity, technology, and nature is in conflict rather than in harmony.

Within solarpunk, it's also important that the goal of sustainability isn't only about technology and the environment. Antiauthoritarianism, cooperation sharing, building resilient communities, anti-imperialism, localism, a DIY spirit, and the struggle against white supremacy and patriarchy are all vitally important characteristics and themes of solarpunk that relate directly to the goal of building a more sustainable society and moving our world toward some semblance of utopia.

SOLARPUNK WITCHCRAFT

As we move through this book, we'll look at the various aspects of our definition of solarpunk in more detail and in relation to the Craft, including many of the above characteristics. Given solarpunk's close relationship to technology, climate science, and even science fiction, it wouldn't be unreasonable to expect people to raise an eyebrow when the idea of a relationship between solarpunk and spirituality is suggested. But this isn't the case. Rather, the attitude I generally find is one of interest, and one that assumes room for spirituality in a solarpunk future.[23]

---

23 There's a new -punk genre called lunarpunk that even seeks to actively and more specifically explore the relationship between spirituality and sustainability as an aspect

So what is solarpunk witchcraft?

If you're already a practicing witch, then you may have already started connecting the dots between solarpunk and witchcraft. And while the notion of any kind of official solarpunk religion is silly and contrary to the diverse spirit of solarpunk, rhetorically speaking, if there were to be an official solarpunk religion, it's Earth-based pagan paths like witchcraft that make a lot of sense.

While there are plenty of differences, solarpunk witchcraft is closely related in many ways to green witchcraft. In fact, for those who are more familiar with solarpunk than with witchcraft, primers on green witchcraft[24] are an excellent starting place for exploration into the Craft from an explicitly Earth-based and relatively environmentalist, or at least conservationist, perspective.

Green witches are particularly concerned with the Earth and nature. They place heavy, though not necessarily exclusive, emphasis in their practice on the magickal and medicinal properties of flowers, herbs, and other plants, as well as plant oils, stones, and other things found naturally occurring in our ecosystems.[25] Indeed, central to most witchcraft traditions is developing a closer relationship with nature as a balance to widespread urbanism and modern technology's dominant presence in our everyday lives. Which is not to say that witches shun technology—not at all. We simply seek and pursue a healthy balance in our lives and in our world.

Solarpunk witchcraft shares these characteristics. Spiritually, solarpunk witches seek to commune with nature, connect with the biome we inhabit, and strengthen our relationship with planet

---

of solarpunk. While still in its infancy, that new genre has developed some. There are various blogs that have begun staking out the terrain of lunarpunk aesthetics. *Solarpunk Magazine* released a lunarpunk-themed issue in November of 2022. In early 2023, Android Press, *Solarpunk Magazine*'s publisher, released *Bioluminescent: A Lunarpunk Anthology*, as well as a lunarpunk novel, *The Inn at the Amethyst Lantern* by J. Dianne Dotson.

24 Such as *The Green Witch* by Arin Murphy-Hiscock.

25 For more, see Jaime Netzer's "What Is a Green Witch?" article at *CrateJoy*: cratejoy. com/box-insider/green-witch-primer.

Earth. In this way, solarpunk witchcraft is really more about our relationship to the Earth than it is about the Sun.

Like other spiritual traditions, solarpunk witchcraft is about building a connection to and a relationship with something larger than ourselves, something that we don't wholly understand. Unlike most other religions though, that something for solarpunk witches— Nature, the planet Earth—even if not completely discovered and understood, is still tangible, knowable, and grounded in a scientific reality. It isn't based on or dependent upon the belief in deities or other beings that are, by definition, beyond our ability to ever fully understand.

Still, even though the primary focus of witchcraft is our relationship with the Earth and our ecosystem, that doesn't mean the Sun isn't important as well. Without the Sun, life on Earth wouldn't be possible. And so the Sun is key to solarpunk witchcraft. In Chapter Four, we'll outline a basic and adaptable ritual for solarpunk witches that utilizes the energy and ideation behind both Sun and Earth.

Like its literary cousin, which is overtly rooted in leftist politics, solarpunk witchcraft is consciously political to a much greater extent than other kinds of witchcraft and magickal practice tend to be. That's not to say that solarpunk is the only branch of the craft concerned with politics and social justice,[26] only that it's on the more overtly political side of the spectrum. In Part Two of this book, we'll not only delve more directly into solar magick and ritual practices for solarpunk witches, but we'll learn new spells rooted in Earth-based activism and the solarpunk ethos. Just as important, we'll also explore practical ways we can work to manifest those spells and create change in the real world around the issues for which we do our spellwork.

It's clear then that while solarpunk witchcraft is a fresh framework, a new tradition in the Craft, there are many witches

---

26 Starhawk's *Reclaiming Tradition*, for example, very much concerns itself with environmentalism and issues of social justice.

who will read this book and think, "Hey, I've been doing this for years!" Indeed, while solarpunk draws on predecessors such as green witchcraft, the Reclaiming Tradition, and others, it also incorporates the addition of solarpunk values and ethos to create a unique tradition and practice.

It will be useful at this point for us to look at some specific characteristics of solarpunk—what they look like and how they translate for us, as solarpunk witches, into a spiritual and magickal practice. For ease of discussion, I've taken a variety of general characteristics of solarpunk and broken them out into three categories that include Vision and Attitude, Sustainable and Equitable Solutions, and Socio-Political Transformation.

Vision and Attitude
This category encompasses the mental, emotional, and ideological mindset that forms the foundational ethos of solarpunk.

Optimism and Radical Hope
Optimism and radical hope are cornerstones of solarpunk, which advocates for a positive outlook, not as a form of naivete or denial, but as a radical act of resistance against pessimism, despair, and environmental destruction. Radical hope involves nurturing a conviction that a better, greener, more just and equitable future is possible, even in the face of adversity. It's about believing that our efforts to fight climate change, build sustainable communities, and create equitable societies will bear fruit. This hope inspires and energizes us as solarpunk witches in our pursuit of transformative change. As a basic value to our Craft, optimism serves as soil from which our spirituality and magickal practice grow.

Utopianism or Non-Dystopian Futurism
In contrast to many modern narratives, solarpunk imagines a future that isn't dystopian, but rather utopian in nature. It's a vision of the future challenging the notion that technology and progress inevitably lead to societal decay. Instead, solarpunk looks ahead

with optimism and hope, envisaging a world where humanity has learned to live in harmony with nature—or at the very least is consciously striving and working to build resilience toward that collective goal. It dreams of a world where technology is used to enhance our relationship with the Earth, rather than exploit it. This ethos shapes our magick, rituals, and daily practices as solarpunk witches, directing our intentions toward creation—toward building a brighter, greener, and more equitable future.

Redefining the Meaning of Comfort and Luxury

Solarpunk narratives reimagine comfort and luxury, which are no longer about excessive consumption and wealth accumulation. Instead, true comfort is found in sustainable living, and luxury is redefined as the ability to live in harmony with nature and our community. For the solarpunk witch, the epitome of luxury and comfort becomes a simple ritual under the Sun, a meal harvested from a community garden, a walk through nature, the ability to breathe clean, unpolluted air, and enjoying time with our loved ones.

Sharing, Compassion, and Empathy

These values lie at the heart of solarpunk's communal ethos. The movement advocates for a compassionate society where resources are shared, and everyone's needs are met. Empathy towards all beings, including the Earth itself, is a vital component of this ethos. In the solarpunk witch's practice, these values manifest in rituals and magick aimed at healing, nurturing, and supporting communities and the Earth.

Skepticism of Hierarchy

Many solarpunks look upon hierarchies with skepticism. The movement promotes more egalitarian and horizontal structures in societies, communities, and relationships. In solarpunk witchcraft, this perspective translates into a practice that values every voice and empowers individuals, while also encouraging collaborative work and decision-making. Hierarchies are flattened, making way for an inclusive and democratic form of spirituality.

Diversity of Political Tactics

Solarpunk recognizes that there's no one-size-fits-all solution to the problems we face. The movement embraces a diversity of tactics— from community organizing and political activism to personal lifestyle changes and magickal workings. Solarpunk witches might engage in a variety of activities to advocate for change, such as casting spells for environmental healing, participating in local sustainability initiatives, using their craft to raise awareness about social issues, or donating money to mutual aid networks. This flexible, pragmatic approach recognizes that all efforts, no matter how small, contribute to the larger goal of creating a sustainable and equitable world.

Sustainable and Equitable Solutions

This category includes both technological and non-technological solutions aimed at addressing climate change, energy use, and resource management. It reflects the solarpunk emphasis on leveraging technology and innovative socio-economic models for creating sustainable futures.

Renewable Energy

In solarpunk, renewable energy is seen not only as an ecological necessity but also as a symbol of hope, autonomy, and resilience. Solarpunk witches often incorporate the symbolism of renewable energy into their practice. They may use the sun, wind, or other natural forces as metaphors or actual sources of energy in their rituals and magick, seeing them as a potent symbol of a future where humanity lives in balance with the Earth.

Ending Fossil Fuels

The transition away from fossil fuels and towards renewable energy is a central tenet of solarpunk. It's a critical step towards building a sustainable and equitable future. Solarpunk witches might incorporate this goal into their magickal practice by focusing their intentions and energy on supporting the transition to clean energy, or by doing work aimed at revealing and reducing the harm caused by fossil fuels. As solarpunk witches, we can also ensure our own practices are as fossil fuel free as possible. One way to do this is by using only soy-based or beeswax candles, rather than the more common paraffin-based[27] candles.

Technological Solutions to Climate Change

While solarpunk recognizes the potential of technology to address climate change, it also acknowledges the importance of using technology responsibly and equitably. As a solarpunk witch, I like to view my magick as a form of spiritual technology, using it to effect positive change and to raise consciousness about the impacts of climate change.

Socio-Economic and Cultural Solutions to Climate Change

Solarpunks understand the climate crisis isn't just an environmental issue—it's also a socio-economic and cultural problem. It calls for systemic change, not just technological fixes. Solarpunk witches incorporate this understanding into their practice by using magick to support social justice movements, or by using their Craft to promote cultural shifts towards sustainability and equity.

Near-Future Reductions in Energy Use

Solarpunk recognizes that in order to avoid the worst outcomes of the climate catastrophe, short term reductions in energy consumption will likely be necessary. And the energy we do use needs to come from renewable sources. We also recognize that reductions in energy consumption have to be undertaken with equity and care to ensure those who are most vulnerable aren't sacrificed. In line

---

27 Paraffin is made by distilling petroleum into wax and is used to make candles as well waterproofing and cosmetics products.

with this, solarpunk witches often focus on magick that promotes conservation, efficiency, and mindfulness of our energy use. Their rituals and spells might aim to shift consciousness towards more sustainable habits and systems.

Creative Reuse and Upcycling

Solarpunk values resourcefulness and creativity, particularly when it comes to reusing and upcycling materials. This ethos can be incorporated into solarpunk witchcraft through the reuse and repurposing of ritual tools, the creation of altars from found items, or the use of upcycled materials in spellwork. This aspect of solarpunk witchcraft serves as a reminder of the value and magic inherent in all things, even those society discards. Of course, it's also important to perform cleansings on such materials to ensure they're washed away of any previous negative associations and energy that might conflict with the hopeful and constructive magickal work you do as a solarpunk witch.

Post-Scarcity Economics

Solarpunk challenges the narrative of scarcity that underpins much of our current capitalist economic system. It recognizes that we've already created a world that produces more than enough for everyone, and the problems of poverty, hunger, and lack of resources are issues of distribution, not of production. Solarpunk then imagines a world where resources are shared equitably and where everyone's basic needs are met. As solarpunk witches, we bring this vision into our magick by focusing our intentions on abundance, equity, and the collective good. We can also use our practice to challenge and transform our own relationships with money, consumption, and value.

Socio-Political Transformation

This category outlines the structural changes solarpunk seeks to promote in society. These changes aim to create more equitable and diverse societies, and to dismantle systems of oppression.

Ending Capitalism, Imperialism, White Supremacy, and Patriarchy

Solarpunk envisions a radical reorganization of society. In its vision, horizontal, equitable, and sustainable systems replace capitalism, imperialism, white supremacy, and patriarchy. In this regard, solarpunk witches see their craft as a form of resistance and transformation. We direct our spells, rituals, and practices toward revealing oppressive systems, healing the harm they cause, and manifesting alternatives. Solarpunk witchcraft can be a powerful tool for personal and collective liberation, providing a way to dream up and work towards a more just and equitable world.

Collectivism, Collaboration, and Cooperation

In resistance to a culture steeped in the value of competition and pitting people, businesses, communities, and nations against each other, solarpunk places a strong emphasis on the values of collectivism, collaboration, and cooperation. This ethos is reflected in solarpunk witchcraft, both in the way rituals are conducted and the intentions behind spellwork. Community rituals, collaborative spell casting, coven and Craft community social organization, and sharing of knowledge and resources—all of these can embody this principle. Solarpunk witches might also focus magickal intentions on fostering cooperation, mutual aid, and community resilience.

Meaningful Diversity and Leadership from Below

Solarpunk celebrates diversity, not just as an abstract concept but as a source of community resilience and strength. It also values leadership from below, recognizing that those who are most affected by an issue are often the ones best equipped to address it. Solarpunk witches incorporate these values into our spirituality in various ways. We aim to create inclusive spaces, both physically and spiritually, where diverse voices are heard and valued. We use magick to uplift marginalized voices, to challenge oppressive power structures, and to support grassroots leadership. In this way, solarpunk witchcraft is a means of manifesting a world where diversity is celebrated and where power is shared equitably.

· · ·

Put most simply, solarpunk witchcraft is a radical magickal and spiritual praxis. It's witchcraft with a focus not only on the Earth and its magick, but also on the use of magick and other spiritual tools in the struggle aid the Earth: to end fossil fuel use, stop climate change, end white supremacy, and establish a solarpunk utopia here in the physical world.

Exactly what this looks like from spell to spell, ritual to ritual, witch to witch, or coven to coven will be different. For some, their entire practice may focus on performing magick in the service of aiding the solarpunk struggle. For others, it may be one part of their larger spiritual and magickal practice. Some may be generalists in terms of magickal methodologies, while others might focus on their use of sigils or candle magick in their solarpunk work. There isn't a right or wrong way to do solarpunk witchcraft in that sense. Rather, it's simply important that, one way or another, we do the work, because there's no doubt about the urgency of our predicament.

The time for us to act is now. And it was yesterday. And it was last year. And it's tomorrow. Whether that action is spiritual and magickal, practical and political, radical and disruptive, or mainstream and legal, we are well past the point where all of the above is the only option that will suffice: we need each other and all of the skills each of us brings. It's my hope that the rituals and spells that follow will aid others in getting involved and carrying out this work.

If we're going to succeed, then it has to be all hands on deck. The time has come for solarpunk witchcraft.

THE FOUR ELEMENTS: EARTH, AIR, FIRE, AND WATER

In solarpunk witchcraft, the four classical elements—Earth, Air, Fire, and Water—are foundational and part of virtually every ritual ceremony. They represent different aspects of the natural world (the Earth) and the human experience, each having its own set of associated characteristics, symbols, and meanings. Each of the four elements is integral to life, and their interplay is considered fundamental to the balance of nature. For solarpunk witches, understanding the spiritual concept of the four elements is central in our quest to build a harmonious relationship with nature.

Earth

In relation to the Earth element, all the elements share a unique, symbiotic relationship: It is both the source and the destination, the foundation of our existence and the material reality we inhabit. It represents stability, strength, abundance, and fertility, reflecting the solarpunk principles of grounding our futurism in tangible, sustainable action and valuing the Earth's resources.

Air

Air is associated with communication, intellect, and new beginnings, reflecting the solarpunk principle of spreading the message of sustainable living and engaging in creative problem-solving to meet our climate challenges. It can be seen as the wind that carries seeds, allowing the potential life within them to find fertile ground within the Earth—and flourish.

Fire

Fire represents transformation, will, and action. Its heat and energy can be seen as a metaphor for the revolutionary zeal that drives the solarpunk movement. Just as Fire changes whatever it touches, solarpunks aim to transform society towards a more sustainable, more equitable, and brighter future. The Earth provides the fuel for Fire, allowing it to exist and perform its transformative work.

Water

Water is linked to emotions, intuition, and healing. It nurtures the Earth, enabling life to thrive, just as empathy and understanding allow communities to flourish. In the solarpunk context, Water can represent the emotional resilience necessary to face the climate crisis and the healing that needs to happen at both personal and global levels.

•   •   •

In essence, each of these elements can be seen as essential aspects of the Earth, interacting in harmony within the natural world. Similarly, they all play a role in the ideals and practice of solarpunk witchcraft. Recognizing these connections helps solarpunk witches ground their practices in a profound respect for the interconnectedness of all life and the urgency of maintaining balance within these relationships.

Chapter Two: Radical Hope, Radical Politics, and Punk Magick

Before we move on to solarpunk spiritual practices and spells, a look at the relationship between radical hope, radical politics, and magick deserves something of its own discussion. Over the years, one question I've heard with some frequency, particularly from those who are discovering solarpunk for the first time, is how a genre that's all about utopia qualifies as punk. It's a fair question. Afterall, aren't punks rude people who listen to loud and angry music? Aren't punks those crude and obnoxious anarchist kids sitting in the gutter with ukuleles and face tattoos, asking for change and leftovers? Even in science fiction literature and fantasy literature, -punk is all about resisting, rebelling, and fighting against corruption even if the odds are insurmountable.

So where's the punk in utopia?

The first part of the answer to that question is, despite its utopian focus, solarpunk is no different than other -punk literary genres in that resistance and rebellion are foundational elements. In his 2014 article, "Solarpunk: Notes Toward a Manifesto," Adam Flynn, one of the early writers and thinkers on the solarpunk genre, asserts that "There's an oppositional quality to solarpunk, but it's an opposition that begins with infrastructure as a form of resistance."[28] This is evident in the genre's focus on dismantling fossil fuel infrastructure in developing and expanding renewable energy infrastructure.

Seven years later, in the summer of 2021, "A Solarpunk Manifesto," was published online by Regenerative Design, a permaculture training, consulting, and design firm. That article places the -punk in solarpunk within the well-established tradition of resistance. "The 'punk' in solarpunk," it says, "has to do with

---

28 hieroglyph.asu.edu/2014/09/solarpunk-notes-toward-a-manifesto

rebellion, counterculture, post-capitalism, decolonialism and enthusiasm."[29] That statement reflects solarpunk's well-established stress on the expected parts of punk: nonwestern cultures and radical, liberatory political theory and praxis.

The last couple words in the above quote—"decolonialism and enthusiasm"— point us in another direction, toward the idea that hope is punk as fuck and is capable of representing the -punk in solarpunk all on its own. In that vein, Regenerative Design's solarpunk manifesto continues: "We are solarpunks because optimism has been taken away from us and we are trying to take it back," and "we are solarpunks because the only other options are denial or despair."

Since we live in a dystopian reality, we're robbed of our optimism and often see hope as naivete. As a result, we're engaged in a struggle to restore that hope, because without it, we can't win. Put more simply: in a world full of despair, hope is an act of rebellion in its own right.

But the hope of solarpunk isn't a naive hope. We aren't talking about blind faith or uncritical *Pollyanna* optimism. Rather, the hope implicit in solarpunk is what University of Chicago philosopher Jonathan Lear termed "radical hope,"[30] and what NYU research professor José Esteban Muñoz argued is a key component of queer utopianism.[31]

So what is radical hope? It's the kind of hope earned through oppression and struggle, and in the face of annihilation, at the hands of seemingly insurmountable force. It's a hope that, faced with cultural or environmental collapse, enables us to keep moving forward day after day, to keep working toward a better world, to keep demanding utopia, and to keep resisting and struggling, even in the face of overwhelming odds.

---

29 re-des.org/a-solarpunk-manifesto

30 Jonathan Lear, *Radical Hope: Ethics in the Face of Cultural Devastation.* (Cambridge: Harvard University Press, 2008).

31 José Esteban Muñoz, *Cruising Utopia: The Then and There of Queer Futurity.* (New York: New York University Press, 2009).

While on the surface this may seem like naive optimism, it's not. Instead, radical hope is the realization that if we're to go on at all, then hope in resistance and radical system change is our only option.

That sure sounds punk as fuck to me.

Radical hope doesn't only fit the punk ethos and drive the activist spirit. It's also an extremely valuable tool for solarpunk witches and the practice of punk magick.[32] There is, in fact, a direct relationship between radical hope and practicing magick.

At its most simple, magick involves four basic steps:

1. feeling a strong, guttural, and visceral desire for something,

2. generating the willpower to make it real,

3. using those feelings to build up a bunch of powerful energy, and

4. focusing that energy into a visualization related to the target of your magickal work.

For witches, radical hope provides a source for the guttural, visceral desire that is fuel, fire, and spark for our magickal spellwork. When your spiritual hope draws its strength from a lifetime of struggle and oppression against insurmountable odds—a reality for most witches—you're more likely to have a deep well of strong feelings, desires, and righteous anger to draw upon when building energy and power for your spells.

And that is the punk magick of radical hope.

---

32 "Punk magick" is a phrase, coined here, to describe activist- and social change–oriented magick.

Chapter Three: The Power of Sun and Earth

*I*n witchcraft, neo-paganism, and similar spiritual traditions, both Sun and Earth have potent and deeply symbolic associations. And while the Sun/masculine and Earth/feminine associations are prevalent in modern neo-paganism and witchcraft, this symbolism isn't universally applicable or historically consistent across all cultures and all times. Like gender itself, the gender attributions of celestial bodies are cultural constructs, and different cultures have historically assigned varied genders to these entities.

For example, in some cultures, the Sun was considered a goddess and the Earth a god, opposing the modern western association. The Japanese Shinto religion venerates the Sun goddess Amaterasu,[33] while the Maori people of New Zealand recognize Tane Mahuta, a male god of forests and birds, symbolizing the Earth.[34] Similarly, the Norse Eddas speak of the Sun goddess Sunna/Sól and the Moon god Mani, flipping commonly held western gender associations.[35]

These variations underline the fluid nature of symbolic representation across different cultures and eras of human evolution, challenging the rigid binary often present in modern-day spiritual discourse. In today's neo-pagan and witchcraft traditions, the assignment of gender to celestial bodies has been influenced by the cultural, social, and patriarchal norms of our modern world. It's a reminder that in our spiritual practices, we should be conscious of and question such constructs, allowing for more inclusive and diverse understandings and explorations.

---

33 For more information on the Sun goddess, Amaterasu, see nippon.com/en/japan-topics/g00748/amaterasu-the-japanese-sun-goddess.html. For more information on the Japanese Shino religion, see asiasociety.org/education/shinto.
34 For more information on pre-Christian Maori spirituality, see tota.world/article/572.
35 For more on Sunna and Mani, see norse-mythology.org/sol-mani.

In modern witchcraft then, the Sun often symbolizes divine masculinity, a source of life, light, and warmth. It signifies consciousness, clarity, and authority. It's associated with a primary god in many traditions,[36] embodying characteristics like strength, virility, courage, consistency, and logical thought. The Sun's daily journey across the sky and its seasonal shift through the year are often viewed metaphorically, reflecting the cycles of seasons and life, of the passage of time. The Sun's seasonal journey is also the basis for the Wheel of the Year and the eight Sabbat celebrations that we'll dive into later.

On the other hand, the Earth in western neo-pagan traditions usually symbolizes the divine feminine, often associated with the goddess. The Earth represents nurturing, fertility, and stability. It's a symbol of abundance, creativity, physicality, and groundedness. It's also associated with the concept of Mother Earth or Gaia, who gives birth to all life and to whom all life one day returns.

The relationship between the Sun and Earth in these traditions often reflects a sacred dance or an eternal romance between the divine masculine and feminine. The interaction between the two represents the dynamic interplay of forces that bring life into existence and sustain it. This idea often appears in rituals and festivals that celebrate the changing of the seasons, celebrate the cyclical nature of life, and, in some traditions, include symbolic sexual intercourse between the divine masculine and feminine.[37]

---

36 Even in Christianity, the Sun is indirectly associated with Yahweh in many ways. For example, Jesus Christ, who is one third of the religion's triumvirate godhead, is known primarily as the *Son* of God and the *Son* of Man. In the famous New Testament biblical passage John 3:16, Jesus even refers to himself as "the way, the truth, and *the light*" who guides his followers to righteousness, i.e. to God. For anyone interested in the connections behind the mythologies of Jesus and other Sun gods, I suggest reading *The Jesus Mysteries: Was the "Original Jesus" a Pagan God?* by Tim Freke and Peter Gandy.

37 This most often takes the form of a priest dipping the athame (ritual knife) into a chalice (ritual cup) held by a priestess. If you're in the Craft (especially if you're femme) and anyone ever tells you that you need to have sex with them as part of your spiritual or magickal education and/or practice, feel free to promptly kick them in the groin and make a speedy exit.

For example, the Wheel of the Year (mentioned briefly above), is a key concept in many neo-pagan traditions. It represents the cycle of the seasons, marked by eight sabbats or holidays. The Wheel reflects the dance between the Sun and the Earth—the solstices and equinoxes mark the key points in the Sun's journey, while the remaining four festivals are tied to the agricultural cycle and the Earth's fertility.

The interdependence of the Sun and Earth reminds us of the interconnectedness of all things and the importance of balance in life. Through honoring these two celestial bodies, we as practitioners learn to balance the divine masculine and feminine within ourselves and in the world around us.

Like in modern western Craft traditions, the Sun and Earth are naturally central figures within utopian, solarpunk witchcraft. Within this budding and radical new Craft tradition, these celestial bodies carry with them a unique symbolism that echoes the core ethos of solarpunk.

THE SUN

The Sun in solarpunk witchcraft can symbolize renewable energy, and even renewable life through the process of reincarnation.[38] The Sun represents hope, resilience, and revolutionary change not only for our societies and communities, but also within each of us more intimately, personally, and spiritually. It's the transformative power of nature harnessed to create a harmonious and sustainable future. And it's the power of the light within each of us to transform, evolve, and grow.

The Sun isn't just an entity to be worshiped or used, but is also a daily reminder of humanity's capability to adapt, grow, and do better. It symbolizes the transition from the use of destructive, fossil fuel–based sources of power to clean, sustainable energy. Harnessing the power of the Sun through solar energy aligns perfectly with

---

38 Regardless of whether you believe in physical or spiritual reincarnation, or both.

the solarpunk ethos of working with nature rather than against it, focusing on self-sufficiency and sustainable development.

THE EARTH

Meanwhile, the Earth in solarpunk witchcraft is conceived as a living entity that is both respected by humanity as well as protected from the consequences of human activity. Earth is not only the provider of resources but also a partner in our journey toward a sustainable future. Earth symbolizes the interconnectivity of all life, emphasizing the need for humanity to live in harmony with nature. It represents the principle of permaculture—nurturing the soil, planting native species, rewilding urban spaces, and designing our habitats to work with the local ecosystems rather than against them.

In the same way, the Earth represents nurturing our own inner soil, planting the seeds of inner change and transformation, and working to help them sprout and grow to harvest. It symbolizes our own struggle to live in harmony with both our exterior and interior ecosystems.

•　　•　　•

In solarpunk witchcraft, the Sun and Earth together create a symbolic representation of the ideal balance between energy production and ecological conservation. Their relationship underlines the solarpunk vision of a future where human societies and technology coexist harmoniously with nature, powered by clean, renewable energy. This symbolism encourages solarpunks to cultivate a sense of responsibility toward both the natural and social environment, instilling a commitment to activism, sustainability, and the pursuit of a better, greener future.

Both Sun and Earth then are equally important in their own ways for the practice of solarpunk witchcraft. Each is infused with its own symbolism, linking the solarpunk ethos to the craft and magickal practice. Each plays a vital role in solarpunk magick in the same way both a god and a goddess are core components for magickal ritual in polytheistic traditions. The Sun and Earth are each woven into the mythos and practice of solarpunk witchcraft in their own unique ways, as well as together, in relationship to one another.

That means that as utopian, solarpunk witches, we work with the energies of both the Sun and Earth in our magickal and spiritual practice. Sometimes we work with them individually, one at a time, and often we'll use them together in the same ritual or spell. Which of the two you work with and when will depend on a variety of factors, like the kind of ritual you're performing and the kind of magickal work you'll be performing during that ritual, among other potential considerations.

A solarpunk witch, as an example, might engage with the Sun's energy in a spell or ritual focused on personal transformation or initiating a new project. At dawn, you could perform a solar invocation, calling upon the Sun's renewing energy to bolster courage, clarity, and drive in your life. You might visualize the Sun's light illuminating your path forward, helping you overcome obstacles to realize your vision. This could be particularly effective at the Summer Solstice, a time of maximum solar power and energy, or during solar flares, which can be viewed as special times of heightened solar energy and thus increased power for solar spells and rituals.

Similarly, you might want to perform an Earth-focused spell in order to ground yourself, cultivate inner peace, or nurture a sense of connection with the natural world. As a solarpunk witch, you might create a small garden—whether in a yard or in planting pots on a city balcony—to connect with the Earth's nurturing and creative energy. As you plant seeds and tend to your plants, you can chant or meditate, channeling your desires into the soil and the plants, trusting in the Earth's capacity to support and nurture growth to fruition. This would be particularly potent either during the autumn, when harvests are brought in, or when planting a new garden in the spring.

A ritual that works with both the Sun and Earth's energies might be performed to symbolize balance, harmony, and interconnectedness, both in your own life and the ecosystem around you. For instance, during an equinox, when day and night are of equal length, you could perform a ritual that honors the vital balance between the solar and terrestrial realms. This could involve an outdoor meditation where you consciously absorb sunlight while also being in contact with the bare Earth. You could then direct this combined energy towards a specific intention, such as promoting balance and harmony within your community or working towards a more sustainable lifestyle.

ASTROLOGY AND WORKING WITH OTHER CELESTIAL BODIES IN SOLARPUNK WITCHCRAFT

We're by no means limited to using the Sun and Earth in our ritual and spellwork as solarpunk witches. While this book will focus on those two celestial bodies and working with their energies, other celestial bodies can be incorporated as well.Below is a brief look at how other planets in our solar system can be woven into your solarpunk spirituality and magickal practice.

Mercury

Mercury traditionally symbolizes communication, intellect, and travel. It's the planet that governs the exchange of ideas, decision-making, and intellectual growth. Within the context of solarpunk witchcraft, Mercury can represent the critical importance of community dialogue, education, and the distribution of knowledge in promoting sustainable practices and eco-consciousness.

Mercury moves around the Sun faster than any other planet, which means two things. One, it goes retrograde from Earth's perspective more than any other planet, and two, out of all the planets, it stays in retrograde for the shortest amount of time. For this reason, astrologers consider Mercury to be swift and adaptable. For solarpunks, this can symbolize the flexibility required to adapt to rapidly shifting environmental conditions that come with climate change, and the ability to make swift but informed decisions in the face of ecological challenges.

A solarpunk spell invoking the energy of Mercury might be performed when launching a new sustainability initiative, aiming to promote open, honest, and effective communication within the team. Alternatively, you might invoke Mercury in a ritual aimed at increasing your own understanding and knowledge of complex environmental issues, thus empowering yourself to contribute effectively to community dialogues on these topics.

Venus

Venus, the planet of love, beauty, and harmony, takes on a special significance within a solarpunk framework. Venus represents the deep love and appreciation for the Earth and its diverse ecosystems, which is at the heart of the solarpunk ethos and values. The planet's association with beauty and harmony can symbolize the inherent beauty of a balanced, thriving ecosystem and the aspiration of solarpunks to create harmonious relationships between our societies, technology, and the natural world.

In a Venus-focused ritual, you might create a sacred space in your garden or home filled with natural, eco-friendly elements of beauty to honor Venus. You might also invoke Venus in a spell to enhance your connection with nature, to deepen your appreciation for the Earth's beauty, or to strengthen your commitment to harmonious, sustainable living. This could involve practices such as crafting natural, eco-friendly art, engaging in mindful walks in nature, or planting and caring for a tree or garden as a symbolic gesture of commitment to Venusian principles.

The Moon

The Moon in traditional modern witchcraft and astrology generally represents intuition, emotions, and the unconscious. It's also associated with cycles and transformation. In the context of solarpunk witchcraft, the Moon holds a special place. Its connection to cycles can be seen as a reflection of the natural rhythms of the Earth and our lives, a reminder of the importance of working in harmony with these cycles in our pursuit of sustainability. The transformation aspect of the Moon mirrors the transitions that our society, our communities, and each of us as individuals need to undergo to live more sustainably and build a better world.

The Moon's association with intuition and the unconscious suggests the need for a deep, intuitive understanding of nature, our own unconscious attitudes toward the environment, as well as our unconscious biases which uphold and feed oppressions driving capitalism, such as systems of white supremacy, patriarchy, and heteronormativity. Similarly, the Moon might also symbolize the nurturing care that we should extend to our environment and to each other, reminiscent of Moon's traditional associations with caregiving and protection.

In a Moon-focused ritual, a solarpunk witch might work to strengthen their intuitive connection with nature or seek guidance for personal transformation towards a more sustainable lifestyle. You could also invoke the Moon's energy to reveal unconscious attitudes or behaviors that are not in alignment with your environmental and social justice values. For example, during a full Moon, you might perform a ritual to release old habits that no longer serve your goal of living sustainably, taking advantage of the full Moon's traditional association with release and completion. On the new Moon, you might plant the seeds for new, sustainable habits, invoking the new Moon's energies of beginnings and intentions. As a solarpunk witch, you could thus work in harmony with the Moon's cycles, reflecting the solarpunk value of living in sync with nature and the natural rhythms of the Earth and life.

Mars

Mars is a planet of action, ambition, and conflict, representing our drive to assert ourselves and achieve our goals. Within the context of solarpunk, this planet becomes a symbol of the courage, determination, and assertiveness needed to advocate for environmental justice and sustainable living. Its association with war and conflict can be seen as the struggle against fossil fuels, corporate corruption, white supremacy, patriarchy, imperialism, and other social ills and unsustainable practices, as well as the need to confront and challenge systems that harm the environment and our communities.

In a Mars-focused ritual, a solarpunk witch could invoke the energy of Mars to empower activism. It could bolster your resolve in the face of adversity, or energize a project aimed at transforming your community towards sustainability. For example, you could perform a ritual before participating in a peaceful environmental protest, asking Mars for the courage to voice your beliefs effectively. Mars can also be invoked in a spell or ritual aimed at resolving conflicts within your community, facilitating a harmonious shift towards more sustainable practices in general.

Jupiter

Jupiter, the planet of expansion, abundance, and wisdom, aligns well with the hopeful, visionary aspects of the solarpunk movement. Jupiter represents the desire to grow, learn, and build a brighter, more sustainable future where everyone is welcome, and where everyone has a valuable voice and role to play. It can symbolize the expansive optimism and hope that underpins the solarpunk vision, inspiring us to believe in the possibility of a green, egalitarian utopia. Jupiter's association with abundance and prosperity can also reflect the bountiful natural resources we have here on Earth, and the need to manage them equitably.

In a ritual inspired by Jupiter, you might focus on expanding your influence in promoting sustainable practices, invoking Jupiter"s energy to bring success to your initiatives. This could be particularly potent when starting a large community project, such as a community garden or local clean energy initiative. Invoking Jupiter could also be useful in rituals aimed at personal growth in areas of sustainability, permaculture, or renewable energy technologies. Jupiter's wisdom could guide you, as a solarpunk witch, in your journey towards becoming a more knowledgeable and effective advocate for the Earth and social justice.

Saturn

Saturn, traditionally associated with structure, discipline, and time, holds a unique role in solarpunk witchcraft. It can symbolize the societal structures and systems that we need to reassess and transform for a more sustainable future. The disciplined aspect of Saturn aligns with the commitment, perseverance, and long-term mindset necessary for true environmental stewardship. Saturn's time element carries a reminder that sustainable transformation, both on a personal and societal level, is a process, not an immediate change.

A solarpunk witch might invoke Saturn's energy in rituals designed to strengthen their commitment to sustainable lifestyle changes or long-term environmental projects. For instance, a solarpunk witch might perform a Saturn-focused ritual at the beginning of a year, setting sustainable goals for the upcoming months and asking for the discipline and fortitude to see them through.

Uranus

Uranus is the planet of change, revolution, and innovation— attributes that sync perfectly with solarpunk's ethos of progressive change towards a greener future. Uranus encourages the breaking of old, harmful patterns and the creation of new, more sustainable ones, symbolizing the innovative technologies and practices at the heart of the solarpunk movement. As a bringer of sudden and unexpected changes, Uranus also reflects the unpredictability of environmental factors and the need for resilience and adaptability in the face of these challenges.

A solarpunk witch might invoke Uranus in a spell designed to spark creative solutions to environmental problems or to inspire revolutionary changes in their community's approach to sustainability. For example, if a solarpunk witch were part of a team developing a new renewable energy technology, they might perform a Uranus-inspired ritual to invoke innovation, breakthroughs, and successful implementation of their project.

Neptune

Neptune symbolizes dreams, illusions, and spirituality in astrology. It invites us to connect with our imaginations and inner worlds, urging us to dream big and explore the realm of possibilities. Within the framework of solarpunk witchcraft, Neptune represents the power of dreams and visions in shaping a sustainable future. It encourages solarpunks to envision a utopian world where harmony with nature is not only possible but is the norm. Neptune's association with spirituality can also highlight the importance of fostering a deep, spiritual connection with the Earth and its diverse ecosystems.

In a Neptune-focused ritual, a solarpunk witch could focus on enhancing their intuition and empathy towards the natural world, fostering a deeper spiritual connection with nature. They could also invoke Neptune's energy to help manifest their visions of a sustainable future. For instance, they might perform a ritual that involves visualizing their dream of a green, sustainable community, asking Neptune to help bring this vision into reality.

Pluto

Pluto stands for transformation, rebirth, and the subconscious in astrology. As such, Pluto can symbolize the profound transformations that need to occur on both a personal and societal level for a truly sustainable future. The planet's association with rebirth is particularly relevant to the cycles of nature and the concept of regeneration, a core principle of sustainable living and permaculture. In terms of the subconscious, Pluto could be linked to the deeply ingrained habits and beliefs we need to change to adopt a more sustainable lifestyle.

In a Pluto-inspired ritual, a solarpunk witch could focus on invoking transformative energy, perhaps as part of a spell for paradigm-shifting personal growth in their approach to sustainability. They might also perform a Pluto-focused ritual to shed light on the subconscious beliefs or habits that are hindering their path towards a sustainable lifestyle, asking for Pluto's transformative power to help them make necessary changes. For instance, a solarpunk witch might use a Pluto-themed ritual to support their transition to a zero-waste lifestyle, symbolically burying their old wasteful habits and celebrating their rebirth as a zero-waste advocate.

•   •   •

As we bring this first section to a close, we've established a solid foundation on which to build our solarpunk, utopian Craft practice.

In Chapter One, we explored some basics of both solarpunk and witchcraft. Then we talked about their shared reverence for nature and the seemingly natural relationship between the two.

In Chapter Two, we touched on the idea of radical hope, a hope rooted in oppressed communities that shines through when you have no other choice but to struggle for a better world. We looked briefly at this concept's influence in solarpunk, and how radical hope can aid us in our magickal activism.

Here in Chapter Three, we delved into the rich symbolism and significance of celestial bodies in relation to solarpunk witchcraft, highlighting their unique roles and energies. The Sun, representing renewable energy, hope, the transformative power of nature, and the potential for personal and communal growth towards a sustainable future. The Earth, a living entity emphasizing interconnectivity and the importance of living in harmony with nature, embodying principles like permaculture and ecological conservation. Other planets, such as Mercury, Venus, Mars, Jupiter, Saturn, Uranus, Neptune, and Pluto, each contribute their distinct energies and symbolisms, from communication and harmony to action, expansion, and transformation. These celestial bodies offer diverse pathways for solarpunk witches to engage with the cosmos, weaving their energies into rituals and practices that reflect the solarpunk ethos of sustainability, balance, and interconnectedness.

Part Two:

Foundations for a Solarpunk Magickal Practice

*T*n astrological, New Age, and magickal traditions, the Sun has important meaning and correspondence for solarpunk witches.[39] The Sun is a fiery planet. As such, it represents the power of passion and inspiration as well as the destruction/creation dichotomy. It also corresponds with growth, vitality, power, generosity, empowerment, and self-confidence. Additionally, the Sun is often associated with a number of characteristics that aren't particularly grounded in solarpunk values: pride, ambition, ego, and wealth. But within a solarpunk context, we can find new meanings in these terms.

Wealth doesn't need to mean having a lot of money or possessions. It could mean being wealthy in community, in spirit, in love, in meaning, and in belonging.

Similarly, ambition in a solarpunk context is about the drive to solve climate change and other global problems. It's the ambition to end capitalism and create a more compassionate and cooperative economic system. It means the active desire to build more resilient and diverse communities.

And pride? For solarpunks, this Sun-associated characteristic invites us to release any attitudes rooted in ego and false pride. We let go of our racism, our speciesism, and other supremacist attitudes. We eliminate national pride, i.e. patriotism, and the imperialist jingoism it fosters. And we check our collective pride as a species and understand our place within our ecosystem so we can build a more healthy and harmonious relationship with nature.

Therefore, even though the primary focus of solarpunk witchcraft is our relationship to the Earth, there is still plenty of reason and room to build a solarpunk spiritual practice that also honors the Sun.

With that in mind, the following chapters contain meditations, rituals, spells, correspondences, and spiritual practices rooted in the

39 For those who want a much deeper dive into the Sun and its symbolism in magickal and astrological terms, one place to start is Mari Silva's *The Sun in Astrology: The Ultimate Guide to the Giver of Life, Its Role in Vedic Astrology, and Sun Sign.*

Sun's physical and spiritual energy and in mythologies that place central focus on the Sun. And since the Earth is also so important to solarpunk witchcraft, Chapter Seven will cover Earth magick's role in this spiritual practice. Part Two also includes a basic ritual for solarpunk witches (Chapter Four).

Chapter Four: A Basic Ritual for Solarpunk Witches

Rituals aren't necessary to perform magick. The two can go hand-in-hand, of course. There are certainly benefits to couching the performance of a spell within a ritual. And there are benefits to a regular ritual practice in and of itself, such as helping the brain shift into sacred magickal space, creating an environment conducive to raise significant amounts of spiritual power, and aiding in focus and the process of physical and mental relaxation. But you can also do magick on the run, so to speak, without any of the preparation or pageantry.

Below is the template for a basic solarpunk ritual. While not entirely different from a non-solarpunk ritual in form, this one is uniquely imbued with solarpunk themes, focus, and intention. If you aren't familiar with a basic craft ritual, this example will more than suffice as a primer and adaptable outline. After we explore this basic solarpunk ritual, we'll jump into examples of the creative ways you can work solarpunk witchcraft into Sabbat celebrations, spells, and more.

BASIC RITUAL FOR SOLARPUNK WITCHES

This ritual outline comes in two main sections. The first is pre-ritual preparation. There are five steps in the pre-ritual preparation process that include determining your purpose, timing, location, composing your ritual, and gathering any magickal tools and other supplies you'll need.

The second section contains the outline itself for a basic solarpunk ritual. There are fourteen steps in this ritual process. That sounds like a lot, but many of the steps don't need to take any longer than thirty seconds to a minute, unless you want them to. You should, of course, feel completely free to modify this in whatever way best suits you, or use it as inspiration to create your own unique ritual.

Pre-Ritual Preparation

Step 1: Figure Out Your Purpose

No, not your life's purpose, though I wish you all the fortune and clarity possible in that journey. Rather, I'm talking about your purpose within the context of the ritual you want to perform.

Why do you want to conduct a ritual? Do you have a solarpunk oriented spell or magickal objective? Are you seeking to strengthen your relationship with nature by celebrating a phase of the Moon or a Sabbat? And if so, do you also have a magickal work to perform that's associated with the solarpunk themes related to that period of time? Or are you simply performing a ritual as part of your daily or weekly spiritual practice and routine?

There's no right or wrong answer to any of the above questions. They're simply there to give you things to think about during your ritual preparation. What's important is making sure your intention is clear in your own heart and mind.

Step 2: Determine Your Timing

Next, decide when to do the ritual. Consider Moon phases, witchy holidays, or maybe a particular astrology event makes sense to consider in timing your ritual.

It's also perfectly okay for mundane considerations to drive your choice of when to perform a ritual. Maybe between work and kids you just don't have the time, energy, or focus during the week, and so you always do your rituals on the weekend regardless of other considerations. That's perfectly okay, and you don't need to take anyone seriously if they try to convince you otherwise.

Step 3: Pick a Location

Decide where you want to perform the ritual. Somewhere quiet and conducive to meditation and focus is generally ideal. It might be in your bedroom, in a large closet, in a special room set up especially for rituals and spiritual practice, out in a forest, on a secluded beach, or in your car. You can also do your ritual in a public place in full view of anyone who walks by. Again, it's entirely up to you. Pretty much anywhere works as long as it works for you.

Step 4: Compose Your Ritual

What are you going to say throughout your solarpunk ritual? You can keep this in your head, you can wing it on the spot, or you can sit down ahead of time and write down the words you want to use during the various steps of the ritual. Then you can read them aloud when the time comes. There's no rule saying you're required to memorize a ritual. Feel free to bring notes into your circle and use them if that's helpful for you.

Step 5: Gather Your Supplies

Now that you've determined your purpose and composed your ritual, it's time to gather the magickal tools and other supplies you'll use. Of course, none of these tools and supplies are necessary. Mental magick requires no ritual, tools, or pageantry, and it's perfectly fine and valid if you choose not to bother.

For those who enjoy using tools and pageantry, this is the time to gather your needed materials. Below are lists of typical altar tools and other supplies you might consider gathering for your ritual. Where you place items on your altar is entirely up to you. A few standard placements you might consider include placing a pentacle in a central place on the altar and placing representations of the four elements in their respective corners. You can find a list of basic altar tools/supplies common in witchcraft in the list below.

Basic Altar Tools

- Athame: a ceremonial knife that is double bladed, but dull, and used for directing energy and casting a ritual circle.

- Pentacle: a pentagram, or five-pointed star, set within a circle. On a witch's altar, it's common to place things such as herbs, incense, and salt on a wooden or ceramic pentacle while blessing them.

- Chalice: a ritual cup often placed in the western quadrant of an altar to symbolize the element of Water.

- Small bowl of salt: used in casting circles, and often placed in the northern quadrant of an altar to symbolize the element of Earth.

- Magick wand: like the athame, the wand is a tool used to direct energy. It's generally used when invoking or evoking deities and the four elements into a ritual circle.

- Candles: ideally made from beeswax or soy wax, rather than from paraffin or other fossil fuel based materials. Candles will serve a variety of purposes on your altar, like general ambiance, recognizing deities/archetypes, and magickal spellwork.

- Incense: often placed in the altar quadrant representing the element of air and used in blessings, purifications, and as part of casting the ritual circle.[40]

- Representations of deities, nature, or symbolic archetypes

- Representations of the four elements: Earth, Air, Fire, and Water

- Cake and ale or some alternative

---

40 You can grow your own Earth-friendly, chemical free, organic, all-natural incense by growing herbs in a garden or in pots, harvesting and drying them, and grinding them up into different blends.

Other Supplies and Magickal Tools to Consider
- Small rocks, extra salt, or something else you can to use physically demarcate your circle if you wish

- A lighter or matches to light candles and incense

- Essential oil(s) for blessings and purifications

- Water for the purification processes

- A besom, or ritual broom, to sweep away negative energy and close your circle at the end of a ritual

- A cauldron to safely burn things in during magickal spellwork

- Your book of shadows with your ritual notes, prompts, or script

- Soft, instrumental music that's conducive to focus and a meditative state

Performing the Ritual

Step 1: Pre-Ritual Grounding Meditation

The inner grove or sacred space meditation[41] is a basic and common visualization practice that all witches should have in their toolbelt, regardless of which tradition they're drawn to. Most witches are taught some version of this early on in their studies. It was the very first Craft meditation I was taught when I was seventeen, and I've been doing this meditation in one form or another during two decades in the Craft. The magick inherent in trees and in communities of trees is an important concept and tool in neo-Druidism, and that theme is reflected in this meditation.

To begin, breathe in, saying to yourself, "Relax."

And as you breathe out, tell yourself, "Relax now."

---

41 I especially like a version of this practice that I found almost a decade ago at The Druids Garden: thedruidsgarden.com/2013/03/24/the-wheel-of-the-year-druidic-holiday-guided-mediation/

Imagine a grove of trees. What does the grove look like? What kinds of trees make up your grove? Are there other plants living in community with the grove? What do the textures of the tree barks, the leaves, and the soil feel like against your skin? How does the forest and the air around you smell? Is it sweet? Musty? Dry? Damp? What sounds do you hear? Who is with you in this grove of safety?

Carry this image with you as you breathe in and out and step into the next part of this ritual.

Step 2: Purify the Space and Yourself

Purify the space and yourself using whatever method you prefer. A typical method used to purify ritual space is to fill your chalice with water, use your athame to dish and stir in a lump of salt, and use the salt water to anoint the space with the elements of Water and Earth. You can do so by moving around the space in a deosil (or clockwise) circle,[42] sprinkling the saltwater around.[43] While doing so, you can silently meditate and focus on the elements of Earth and Water, and on the intention of purifying the space, or you can repeat something along the lines of the following:

With salt and sea, in love and peace,
in cooperation with creatures and spirits
of Earth and Ocean, I bless this space.

Next, use a lighter or matches to light incense. Then, in the same way as you did with the elements of Earth and Water, move in

---

42 *Deosil* is another Scottish word that's been widely adopted and used in modern witchcraft. Related to the opposite term *widdershins, deosil* means to move East to West in the direction of the sun. Living at such northern latitudes, people in Scotland generally follow the Sunby looking south. Therefore, moving East to West is the same as moving left to right, or in other words, clockwise.

43 Many witches move around the circle three times when performing ritual or doing magickal work, but once is enough if that's all you want to do, or if moving around the circle is challenging for you due to accessibility issues. Taking that even a step further, if moving around your magickal circle at all presents accessibility issues for you, such movements can be made just as effectively through mental visualization while remaining still in one spot within the circle.

a deosil circle around the space to bless it with the elements of Fire and Air. Again, as you move around the space, you can silently meditate and focus on the task, or you can say something like the following:

With Fire and Air, in love and peace,
in cooperation with creatures and spirits
of Flame and Sky, I bless this space.

You can purify yourself using the same method you used for purifying the space, or another method of your choosing. Other common elements of self-purification include taking a ritual bath and using essential oils to anoint yourself (or each other if you're doing a group ritual).

A note on sage:

I'm putting this right here in the main body of text because I believe it's that important. Sage is a wonderful plant. I grew up wandering the hills of rural Southern California picking white sage leaves, wrapping them in fishing line, hanging them to dry, and regularly burning them just because I love the smell. But white sage in particular is an important and sacred plant to Indigenous peoples in Southern California, which is the only place in the world where the plant is native. In recent years, they've pointed out the cultural appropriation central to the widespread use of sage by white neo-pagans, and how the practice significantly threatens white sage in the wild. They've pointed out dozens of other plants, flowers, and herbs we can use in our rituals instead. They have asked us not to use white sage, to leave it for them.[44]

Each individual is, of course, free to choose whether or not to heed that request. But I encourage solarpunk witches to do so. As colonizers on stolen land, we and our ancestors have already taken

---

44 To learn more about the request that we stop using white sage, see Haley Lewis's *Huffpost* article "Indigenous People Want Brands to Step Selling Sage and Smudge Kits," from November 30, 2018: huffpost.com/entry/indigenous-people-sage-and-smudge-kits_n_610874f5e4b0497e67026adb.

so much from the Indigenous people who were here long before us. It's important to remember that solarpunk isn't only about solving climate change. Just as important to building utopia is ending imperialism, patriarchy, and white supremacy. A racist utopia is no utopia at all. As such, a solarpunk witch who isn't also a member of an Indigenous community is likely—without much of a second thought—to respect the request to refrain from using sage in their spells, rituals, and spiritual practice.

Step 3: Cast a Sacred Sun Circle

In modern witchcraft, a magickal circle is a sacred, purified space in which we perform our rituals and spells. It's a boundary between the mundane world and the spiritual realm, a space where the witch can safely interact with the divine (whatever that means for each individual) and the magickal energies they're working with.

The circle has multiple symbolic meanings. Firstly, it represents a boundary, creating a protected and consecrated space to perform magick safely. The circle keeps negative or disruptive influences at bay, allowing us to focus our intention and energy. It creates a space where we can play, be silly, and be creative without inhibition.

The circle also symbolizes wholeness and infinity. It reminds us of the interconnectedness of all things and the cyclical nature of life, death, and rebirth. In this sense, it's not just a protective boundary but also a container for the energy raised during the ritual or spell.

But why would you want to contain such energy rather than releasing it into the universe? First, you want to contain the power you raise in ritual in order to bring that energy to a climactic peak and use it in performing your magickal work. As part of that magickal work, witches generally use some kind of method to release that energy—while it's at its peak, at its strongest—into the ether, in order to help the magick manifest in the physical realm.

Casting a circle is key to many witchcraft practices. Though the specific circle-casting methods may vary between different traditions and practitioners, the general idea is the same. Cleanse the space (using methods such as smudging with herbs or incense, sprinkling with salt water, or sweeping with a besom), then outline the circle's boundary, and seal it closed inside yourself (and anyone else there, if you're doing group magick). You'll find a more detailed description of how to cast a circle below.

Once your circle is cast, it becomes a working space for your solarpunk ritual or spell. Remember, the use of a magickal circle isn't a requirement in all witchcraft traditions or for all witches; some may prefer to work without a formal circle, especially if their practice is more informal or spontaneous.[45] However, for those who do use them, circles can provide a powerful framework for entering a magickal mindset and focusing your magickal work.

Casting a Circle

To cast a circle, point your athame (or finger) out in front of you at chest level. Walk a deosil circle around the ritual space, making sure the circle is large enough to perform the ritual and whatever work you're planning to do. While walking the circle, imagine the powerful and pure light of the Sun beaming down, solar flares reaching out toward you, like the arms of the universe.

The powerful light pours into you through the open aural crown[46] above your head, a plasmatic energy that flows through you,

---

45 For example, kitchen witches use whatever tools are available and handy at the moment they need them. In that spirit, kitchen witches don't often bother with the formalities of more involved ritual magick. Another example is the practice of mental magick, which is done entirely within the mind through visualization, without the use of physical tools, aids, and trappings of more physically active rituals.

46 For those who may be new to witchcraft and other New Age spiritual philosophies or practices, an aura is conceived of as layers of unseen light surrounding our bodies, and those layers are manifestations of your inner vibrational energy. Chakras, taken from Hindu philosophy, are energy centers thought to be vertically aligned throughout the body from head to feet, and are believed to be closely associated with one's aura. It's said that if our chakras are blocked for any reason that our aura may appear dim and less vibrant. The crown chakra is the chakra at the very top of your head. So the term aural crown refers to the section of aura at the top of your head, and an open aural crown refers to the aura and chakra above your head being open and receptive to the intake of energy. A good resource to begin learning about chakras within their

down your arm, to your fingers, and into your athame, ready to be directed. As you move around the space, use this light to draw your ritual circle in the sacred realm. If you want to say some words, consider something like the following:

I cast this circle in love and cooperation with the creatures and spirits of Sun and Sky.

Step 4: Grounding and Relaxing

When doing magickal work, it's best to be as relaxed as you can be. That doesn't mean you can't ever draw upon the power of righteous indignation in the course of the magickal work, but, going into that work, it's generally best to be in a state of relaxation. It's easier to focus when you're relaxed than when you're tense.

Close your eyes and focus.

Take three long, deep breaths from all the way down in your gut. As you breathe in through your nose, tell yourself, "Relax." As you breathe out through your mouth, tell yourself, "Relax now."

Continue breathing, and relax all the muscles in your body. Go section by section from your feet to your ankles, to your shins, then your knees, and so on, up to the top of your head. As you move through each section of your body, tense up the muscles in that area, hold for a count of three, then release the tension, allowing your body to sink deeper into physical relaxation.

As you breathe deeply, breathe in the light of the Sun and let it fill your body.

Let that light calm and continue to relax you. As you exhale, visualize any sadness, frustrations, anger, or tension you may carry, as they flow out on the wind of your warm exhalations, helping you relax even further.

Continue breathing in the sun, and visualize roots growing out of the bottom of your spine extending down into their Earth.

Hindu context is "A Beginner's Guide to Chakras" at Yoga Journal: yogajournal.com/practice/yoga-sequences-level/beginners-guide-chakras/.

Allow the energy of the Sun to continue filling you. See it flowing through you and your roots and down Earth, creating a singular smooth flow of energy between the Sun and the Earth, with you as a conduit. Your connection to the Sun and Earth grounds you, balances you, relaxes you, centers you.

Continue breathing deeply and relaxing, finding your place of balance between Sun and Earth until you feel ready to proceed.

Step 5: Call the Quarters

Calling the quarters is a practice in many forms of modern witchcraft where the witch calls upon the energies or beings associated with the four cardinal directions—North, South, East, and West. These directions are associated with the four classical elements of Earth, Fire, Air, and Water, respectively. The specific correspondences between the directions and elements can vary depending on the tradition or individual practitioner's preference.

For example, the neo-Druidic tradition I was a member of in my twenties uses a different correspondence system where the elements associated with South and East are swapped, so South corresponds with the element of Air, and East corresponds with Fire. The reasoning behind this, according to that tradition, is that East is the direction the Sun (which has fairly obvious associations with Fire) rises. This is the correspondence I continue to use to this day. As such, it's the way you'll find it here in this book. But you're always free to associate any of the four cardinal directions with whichever of the four elements makes most sense to you personally.

The purpose of calling the quarters is to draw the energies associated with these elements into the ritual and establish a balance of powers within the magickal circle. Each quarter represents different types of energy, and calling upon them helps to ensure a balance of these forces in the work that's about to be done. The ritual can also serve as a means to ask for protection and guidance from these forces or, if you wish, the spiritual beings associated with them.

The act of calling the quarters typically involves facing each direction in turn, starting most often with either the North or the East (depending on the tradition), and using a spoken invocation to call upon the energies or magickal beings of that direction. Here is an example of what you could say in an invocation for each direction and element:

Powers of the East—element of Fire—passion and creativity, join me in this circle.

Powers of the South—element of Air—breath of life and reason, join me in this circle.

Powers of the West—element Water—emotion and intuition, join me in this circle.

Powers of the North—element of Earth—stability and comfort, join me in this circle.

You might also visualize the energy of that element or direction coming into the circle, and use a wand to draw a pentagram (or some other symbol associated with that element and direction) in the air.

After the magickal work is done and before the circle is closed, the witch usually thanks and releases each of the quarters, often in the reverse order in which they were called. This is seen as a sign of respect and a way to restore balance after the ritual.

Step 6: Song to the Earth

At this point in the ritual, many witches evoke, invoke, or welcome deities, often a god and a goddess. Others welcome the universe, symbolic archetypes, or whatever feels appropriate according to their beliefs. You can do so using a prayer, a poem, a song, a few quick words of welcome, through quiet focus of intention, or whatever other way feels right to you personally.

However, in solarpunk, we like to be as inclusive as possible. Many solarpunks and solarpunk witches are agnostics or atheists, and just as many aren't. Again, feel more than free to call deities if you want, but the following is a substitute that for me, feels more solarpunk than calling deities: a song to the Earth.

Solarpunk is about—in no small part—rebuilding our relationship with nature, with the Earth. It's about doing our best to build communities in harmony with nature. The "Song to the Earth" portion of this ritual is a recognition that this planet is sacred and that we're dependent upon it for our birth, life, and survival and that it's where we'll return upon our death. It's a song of honor and respect for the Earth as our home, our comfort, our protection, and our sustenance. It's a recognition that the Earth is a much larger whole, of which we're only one small part.

Personally, I like to use a song called, "Return to the Womb," written by Leora Havah Sarachek. It's a song about how, when we're alone or afraid, we can return to Mother Earth for comfort and safety. I've been singing this song with other pagans since I was a teenager, and it has a lot of personal meaning for me. But I also use one of my own that I wrote a number of years ago called "Song to the Earth," which you'll find the lyrics for below. Of course, as with everything else in your practice of solarpunk witchcraft, feel free to use a different song or write your own.

"Song to the Earth"

Beneath the sky so wide, where winds and dreams collide,
Upon this soil we strive, Earth's heartbeat as our guide.
A chorus in the trees, whispers in the leaves,
Bound in time and space, cradled in Earth's embrace.

We sing to the Earth in joy and in mirth,
Your power we invoke, like the spring newly woke.
From the mountains to the sea, in your love, we are free,

In this circle we unite, in your sacred rite.

Rooted deep and strong, to this land we belong,
In the rock and in the clay, your wisdom points the way.
You hold the secret seeds to meet our deepest needs,
In your cycles without end, our ally and our friend.

We sing to the Earth, acknowledging your worth,
Bearing witness to your might in the day and in the night.
From the river to the tree, in your embrace, we are free,
In this circle, we find grace, within your sacred space.

Blessed Be.

Step 7: Ritual Observance

If you're celebrating a Sabbat (one of the eight seasonal festivals on the Wheel of the Year), an Esbat (full Moonritual), or doing some other kind of ritual observance other than performing magick, this is the time in the ritual to do it. See Chapter Five for examples of solarpunk Sabbat and Esbat observances.

Step 8: Raising Power

During a ritual, we'll raise a cone of power to be channeled as fuel for our magickal spellwork. You can raise a cone of power using the following guided meditation (or creating one of your own).

Close your eyes and take three big, deep breaths. As you breathe in, see light coming into your body and relaxing you. As you breathe out, see all the tension and frustration in your life slipping away and the wind of your breath. Once you feel ready, and as you continue breathing deeply, visualize two roots extending down out of the base of your spine. These roots dive into the waiting, welcoming soil of the Earth and burrow their way down.

Continue breathing as the roots sink farther and farther into the Earth. Finally, watch the roots burst through the final layers and into the central core of the planet. The roots sink gently and smoothly in the Earth's metallic core. Now, as you continue breathing, imagine the energy of the Earth being drawn up through your roots. With each breath, the essence of the Earth rises and rises up through its own body until it reaches yours. With your next breath, feel that energy surge into you and fill your entire being.

Continue breathing until the energy bursts out of the top of your aural head and begins to spill over and around you. As it covers you and fills the space around you, observe the energy begin to circulate deosil around your sacred circle.

As you continue to breathe deeply, let the power of your breath and the force of Earth's energy circulate around you like a vortex—a blackhole drawing down the light, energy, and power of the Sun. With each breath, imagine Earth energy swirling around you, reaching up into the sky further and further. Also with each breath, envision the light of the Sun swirling and descending with greater and greater force.

Finally, with one last deep breath, feel the power of the Earth and Sun collide, merge, blend, and become one in a magickal cone of power that extends from the depths of the earth, up through you, and into the reaches of space and the solarpunk system.

Step 9: Perform Solarpunk Magick

Now that you've raised a cone of power, you're ready to work your solarpunk magick in service of the Earth, humanity, and building utopia. This is the time to perform your spell, whatever that entails. See Part Three for examples of spells you can use or modify to suit your needs.

Step 10: Blessing and Gratitude

Give thanks to the Earth (and/or whatever higher power or archetypes you welcomed into the circle). You can simply say thank you to express gratitude. Another common practice is to have a piece of cake, bread, or fruit and some ale, meade, wine, water, or juice in your chalice (whatever is your preference). Give gratitude for the bounty of the Earth by eating from the food and drinking from the chalice while focusing on your gratitude. Of course, if you're able to, use organic food and drink, grown, produced, and distributed in as sustainable a way as possible.

However, keep in mind that there is no ethical consumption under capitalism. Exploitation is built into the system, and it exists throughout the supply chain. Organic and responsible food is made purposefully expensive by that very same system. Not everyone can afford it. No one should feel ashamed about using what is available to them.

Step 11: Release and Ground the Power

You can do this fairly simply by sitting on the floor with hands on the ground. Visualize the cone of power spinning down from the sun, back down through your body, and into the Earth from where it came. This only takes a minute or two to perform, though you can certainly take longer if you wish. Either way, it's important to ground the energy you raised during your ritual, or else later on you may feel out of balance, jittery, or exhausted.

Step 12: Thank the Earth

Thank the Earth for its abundance, its power, its life force. You can also give thanks to the Earth for anything else you're grateful for to our planet, especially as relevant to the work you did during the ritual.

As always, you can do this in whatever way feels right to you for the moment. You can sit quietly and thank the Earth in your mind or through a visualization. You can say a few simple words of gratitude, recite a pre-written poem, sing a song, or use some other creative method you devise.

Step 13: Thank the Elements

Thank the elemental representations or spirits for each of the four quarters in whatever way feels right to you. You can move widdershins[47] around the circle and say words of departing thanks for each element, and you can use your wand to close the pentagram portals in whatever way seems right. Or you can simply thank them all at the same time with a few quick but heartfelt words.

Step 14: Open the Circle

Point your athame (or finger) out in front of you, arm straight. Walk around the circle widdershins and visualize the circle of sunlight dissolving into a mixture of particles and waves as it gently ascends home into the heart of the Sun.

Next, take your besom to sweep away the remaining energy along with any salt, rocks, or other materials you used to physically demarcate your circle, if any.

•　　　•　　　•

You've now completed a basic solarpunk witchcraft ritual.

---

47 *Widdershins* is a Scottish word that means traveling in a direction opposite the sun, in other words, counterclockwise. The word has been widely adopted into Craft and neo-pagan ritual practices.

Chapter Five: Solarpunk Celebrations—Sabbats and Esbats

Sabbats are among the main festivals celebrated by pagans and witches. Pagan Sabbats fall along the eight spokes of the Wheel of the Year,[48] which follows the solar calendar and is rooted in solar mythology. In global solar mythology, most Sun deities are assigned male gender. There's no doubt a book's worth of historical and anthropological reasons for that, which is well beyond our scope in this book. What's important to recognize is that while male Sun deities may be the norm, it's not an exclusive rule. Some Sun deities were assigned female gender. The Norse deity Sol, for example, is a Sungoddess who rides a horse drawn solar chariot.[49] Also from the furthest richest of Northern Europe, the Saami goddess Beiwe is a Sun deity.[50] In the spirit of solarpunk's inclusivity, I use gender neutral pronouns as much as possible when speaking of deities, as I have throughout this book.

For Wicca in particular, solar mythology follows this cycle called the Wheel of the Year mentioned above. The Wheel is a mirror reflecting Nature's cycles of life and the passing of the seasons into death. The mythological Sun deity is born at Yule, the longest night of the year, after which the days begin getting longer and the Sun begins to grow stronger. At Imbolc, the Sun is a young child. And as the Wheel turns to Ostara, the Spring Equinox, the Sun is a growing youth—a young spring flower beginning to bloom.

Come Beltane, the Sun is a vibrant young adult, and, by Summer Solstice, also called Litha, the Sun deity has reached the mature or parental stage of life. As the Wheel continues turning and

---

48 For more information and historical context about the Wheel of the Year, a good place to start is this online primer at *Word History Encyclopedia*: worldhistory.org/Wheel_of_the_Year

49 thoughtco.com/sun-gods-and-sun-goddesses-121167

50 littlewomen.medium.com/beaivvi-the-sun-goddess-of-the-s%C3%A1pmi-dc092aefd77d

approaches Lammas, the deity becomes a protector and a sacrifice.[51] By Fall Equinox, often called Mabon, the Sun has become an old and wise teacher, living their final days until embraced by the welcoming arms of death at Samhain. Then, when Yule brings us back around the Wheel to Winter Solstice, the Sun deity is reborn, like they have been so many times before, and the Sun begins the cycle anew.

This larger cycle reflects a microcosm of a single day as well. Generally speaking, the Sun rises and grows in strength and heat as it comes to its zenith around midday. It then descends slowly toward dusk and the coming night, only to rise again the next morning. In the spirit of this cycle, we'll now discuss solarpunk celebrations of the Sabbats.

Before moving on to the next section below, ground and center yourselves with your sacred grove meditation. Once you've finished, return here and we'll go through the Sabbats together, considering how these solar festivals relate to our spiritual work as solarpunks, to our solarpunk witchcraft.

SOLARPUNK SABBATS

Eight Sabbats make up the spokes of the Wheel of the Year, celebrated as the main ritual festivals in paganism and the Craft, particularly Wiccan strains of the Craft. The basic ritual format for solarpunk Sabbats is essentially the same as the basic ritual for solarpunk witches outlined in Chapter Four.

The only difference is that you will probably gear each part of the ritual—the language you use to cast your circle and welcome

---

51 The deity/archetype evoked during Lammas is that of the perennial dying god who is sacrificed in order to ensure a good harvest and the health of the community. In the neo-Druidic tradition I first studied under, every year we constructed an effigy out of the fruits and vegetables of the first harvests from our summer gardens. At the center of this effigy was a wicker basket, and, during the Lammas ritual, we placed small sacrifices of grain into the basket. The grain was imbued with the energy of our intentions for the things we wanted to get rid of in our life, and the things we wanted to harvest, or invite and cultivate in our lives. Then, we put the effigy in our central fire pit and burned it.

the elements, as well as any decorations, color schemes, and other correspondences you might use—toward the particular Sabbat you're celebrating. Similarly, the magickal work you'll do during the ritual will likely fit within the themes of that festival and season. But the structure and scaffolding of the ritual will generally be the same.

There are two kinds of work you can do during any ritual, including Sabbats: internal work and external work. Because Sabbats are often group community events, they often focus on an element of external work. I've been to many Sabbat celebrations, though, that also incorporated more personal considerations into the ritual work. So like most things in the Craft, there's no hard and fast rule.

Another way to frame this internal-external dichotomy is personal work and community or social justice work. Of course those dichotomies are illusions. The world is rarely that binary, if ever.

But generally, internal work is work you do on or for yourself. It can include personal, physical, or material needs and desires such as a better job or a new car to replace the one that's going to break down on the highway any day now. This work also includes cultivating personal growth to become a better and more balanced person.

Internal work isn't selfish. We all need and want things, and that's okay. We should always do our best to be personally and socially conscious, to be responsible about our desires and how we go about attaining them. But solarpunk isn't primitivist or ascetic. There's no such thing as ethical consumption or ethical living under capitalism. We can do our best, but, by design, the system forces us into failure in this regard, which is why system change is so important.

There's even overlap between personal, internal work and social justice work. Perhaps you desire new art supplies you can't afford. You want those supplies because there's a big climate march coming up and you really want to make signs for you, as well as extras for others to use. That work clearly falls into the personal, community, and social justice categories of magickal work. As another example, maybe the work you do during your ritual is simply about strengthening your relationship with nature, your ecosystem, and the Earth. In its own right, this strengthening also aids social justice because it inspires you to tangible action in the "mundane" world.

Solarpunk witches then shouldn't be afraid to do magickal work for themselves in addition to their social justice work. Just be socially conscious, environmentally conscious, and responsible. In other words, be a solarpunk.

External work, on the other hand, is work you do for others, for your community, or for the planet. Again, while these aren't necessarily always the same thing, there's an incredible amount of overlap between each of the three kinds of external work. And if you're doing work for your community or the planet, chances are it can somehow fit within the category of social justice, solarpunk work.

Because of the structural similarity of the rituals to the basic ritual outlined in Chapter Four, we also won't go through the entire ritual for each Sabbat celebration. But we'll go through the important basics of each, talk about them in relation to the solarpunk ethos and values, and give some examples of solarpunk magickal work that can be done as a part of each festival.

Winter Solstice/Yule

Winter Solstice is the day of the year in which the daylight is shortest, and the cold, dark of night is longest. Starting the following day, the days begin to slowly but surely get longer again, as if the Sun and its creative, lifegiving light were reborn on the Winter Solstice and are beginning to grow. For this reason, winter is considered a time of birth and rebirth. Solstice celebrations are laden with related symbolism.

It's not hard to imagine how important this day would have been for humans in pre-industrial, agrarian societies. They depended on the Sun in ways most of us in the modern western world don't fully understand. For them, the return of the Sun meant that warmth would soon return. Soon animals would be mating and life would spring forth from the Earth. Food would be more plentiful again.

The solarpunk movement focuses on envisioning and striving for a sustainable, equitable future, and, therefore, the celebration of the Winter Solstice or Yule can hold deep significance. As mentioned above, the Winter Solstice marks the shortest day and longest night of the year, symbolizing the triumph of darkness over light. And it's also the turning point where the days begin to grow longer, signaling the return of light and warmth. This is where the seemingly perennial mythologies about the birth of the Sun have their foundations—divine beings come as "light" to bring some kind of new or necessary knowledge to the world. In many pagan traditions, Yule is a time of introspection and hope for the return of the sun.

This spectrum of darkness and light, of introspection and hope, fits well with the solarpunk vision. Solarpunk acknowledges the environmental and social challenges we face (the long night), while also maintaining a focus on solutions and a brighter, sustainable future (the return of the sun).

Moreover, the Yule celebration traditionally involves practices such as feasting, gift-giving, and decorating homes with symbols of light (like candles or Yule logs) and greenery (like holly or mistletoe). These serve as reminders of nature's resilience even during the coldest and darkest winter nights, as well as the potential for renewal and regeneration—themes that resonate strongly throughout solarpunk communities.

For example, a solarpunk might celebrate Yule by gathering with their community around a bonfire powered by renewable wood sources, sharing a potluck meal of locally-sourced and plant-based foods, exchanging handmade or recycled gifts, and discussing plans for new sustainable projects in the coming year. The emphasis on community, sustainability, and resilience in these celebrations aligns with the solarpunk ethos.

Additionally, the work you do on this day could be as simple as reading or telling old mythological tales of birth and rebirth, such as that of deities like Osiris, Dionisys, Izanami, Odin, or the Holly and Oak spirits.[52] Then you can meditate on—and, if you're working with a group, discuss—the mythology's connection to nature, the winter season, the Wheel of the Year, your communities, or your own individual lives. What lessons do the stories hold for us about ourselves, the Earth, and our relationship to nature?

One common tradition during Winter Solstice celebrations involves lighting fire or candles. While doing so, visualize the winter Sun rising strong and bright from the eastern horizon. In this way, you symbolically or magickally connect with and help encourage the return of the Sun, its warmth, and its life-giving light. Like the above storytelling, meditation, and discussion suggestion, this fire/candle magick can strengthen our connection to Earth and the seasonal cycles of nature, which aids in the overall creation of a more harmonious relationship between humanity and nature.

The above fire magick is an example of internal work. You can easily tailor it into more external kinds of solarpunk magick. At its most simple, that can be done by focusing not only on the rebirth of the Sun, but on the renewal of the Earth, the birth of Earth-centered consciousness, the decline of anthropocentrism, and the rebirth of radical movements capable of creating the systemic changes needed for us to avoid the worst of potential climate disaster.

---

52 Traditionally, they're referred to as the Oak King and the Holly King. I use *Spirit* in place of *King* as a gender neutral alternative.

Celebrating the Winter Solstice or Yule within the context of solarpunk can provide a meaningful way to honor the cycles of nature, acknowledge the challenges ahead, and affirm commitment to a sustainable future. The turning of the seasons serves as a tangible reminder of the constant change and adaptation inherent to both nature and the solarpunk vision.

Imbolc

Moving through the calendar chronologically, the next pagan Sabbat is Imbolc, celebrated on the first or second day of February, halfway between the Winter Solstice and Spring Equinox. Being a Winter Sabbat, Imbolc includes the themes of birth and rebirth, just like at the Winter Solstice. In Celtic tradition, the day is closely associated with the Celtic goddess Brigid and thus is often called Bride's Day.[53]

By this time, the days are noticeably longer. As such, Imbolc is a time when pagans and witches celebrate the manifestation of the reborn Sun in our tangible lives. It's a time to celebrate the growing, strengthening daylight and warmth—of new beginnings and initiations. Seeds—buried within the soil and will later sprout and grow—begin to stir from their dark sleep. And so we witches meet to share the light of inspiration, which will grow with the year.

In the context of solarpunk, Imbolc's theme of renewal aligns perfectly with the movement's focus on creating a new, sustainable future. Imbolc can serve as a reminder of the potential

---

53 Brigid is the goddess of fire, poetry, healing, childbirth, and unity. She is a figure of light and inspiration, embodying the power of creativity and the promise of new life. During Imbolc, which falls at the midpoint between the Winter Solstice and Spring Equinox, the first signs of spring are starting to emerge, and Brigid becomes a potent symbol of the potential within the Earth that is ready to bloom. Traditionally, it's a time to invite her blessings for the coming season's growth. For solarpunk witches, invoking Brigid's energy could be used for sparking creative solutions, fostering unity in community efforts, and rejuvenating personal and collective endeavors. Whether it's through lighting candles in her honor, crafting a Brigid's cross, or dedicating acts of healing and creativity to her, the essence of Brigid is deeply woven into the tapestry of Imbolc.

for adaptability, growth, and change both in ourselves and in our societies. As the Earth begins to wake up from its winter slumber, so too can we awaken to new possibilities and paths toward a more sustainable and equitable future.

The association of Imbolc with the goddess-archetype Brigid also holds potential symbolic significance for solarpunks. Brigid's domains of healing and smithcraft can symbolize the work solarpunks are doing to heal our planet and craft new, sustainable technologies and ways of living. It can also represent solarpunk's DIY ethos. And as a goddess of poetry, Brigid reminds us of the importance of stories and vision in creating a better future.

A solarpunk Imbolc celebration might involve a community gathering to share seeds and gardening tips for the coming growing season, a ritual to bless solar panels or other renewable energy sources, or a poetry reading where participants share their visions for a sustainable future. Such activities would serve to reinforce the connection between the natural cycles of the Earth and the work solarpunks are doing to create a more sustainable world.

If you're doing a group celebration and work, then the spiral dance is a common activity at Imbolc gatherings. In fact, I don't recall ever attending an Imbolc celebration that didn't include a spiral dance. If you don't know how to do the spiral dance, I suggest Starhawk's book by the same name, which is basically unofficial required reading for modern day witches anyway. In it, she does a great job of describing the dance and how it's performed.

Basically, everyone in the circle joins hands, the dance facilitator breaks hands with the person on their right, and begins moving deosil, or clockwise, in an inward leaning circle that creates a spiral of moving bodies. When they can't move inward anymore, the lead person reverses course into a widdershins, or counterclockwise, circle that unwraps the spiral.[54] Light candles when you finish the spiral, then engage in ecstatic dance while focusing on the

---

54 If you're performing a spiral dance during the waning part of the year, like at an Samhain ritual, you'll start the spiral dance widdershins and unwind deosil.

inspiration and creativity you want to bring into your lives over the coming year. Then, place the candles in the central cauldron.

You can easily rework this same dance magick into a more solarpunk style of magick. Participants can focus more specifically on the inspiration and creativity you'll bring to social movements over the coming year. You could also focus your energy and intention on germinating the seeds of system change, or solutions to climate change and other global social problems.

If you're celebrating Imbolc individually, you can perform magickal work with similar intention on your own. You can still do the above dance magick. You'll need to remove the spiral dance part, or you can dance along a spiral-like path. Either way, one individual solarpunk witch can easily do the second, ecstatic dance section.

As an alternative, you can write down on a piece of parchment one or more ways you want to bring inspiration and creativity into your community over the coming year. Raise a cone and focus energy and intention into the parchment and the words and/or symbols written on it. Visualize that inspiration and creativity and channel the power of that visualization into the parchment. Then, burn it in your cauldron fire—which represents the fire, power, and light of the Sun—to activate the spell.

Spring Equinox/Ostara

Spring is a time of fertility, life, and growth. On Earth, all of this is dependent upon the light and energy of the Sun. As the Sun grows, light grows in length and strength throughout the winter. The Sun combines with Water to feed the seeds stirring just beneath the soil's surface. Those seeds, and the plant life that springs forth from them, use the Sun's light and Water to create energy and fuel through photosynthesis.[55] Then animals eat those plants for fuel,

---

55 If you're not familiar with, or want to brush up on the science behind photosynthesis is, the Smithsonian's Science Education Center's site is a great resource meant for a broad audience: ssec.si.edu/stemvisions-blog/what-photosynthesis.

and animals also eat each other as well. It's the basic web of life.[56] And it all starts with the Sun as one of the primary and necessary components.

In nature, the first flowers are coming to life and soon they'll be a sea of blooming and pollinating. Late winter and early spring mating seasons will bring new generations of animal life which will grow with each passing beautiful spring day. Seeds on most farms and in most gardens—with the exception of more northern and southern regions that are further from the equator—have been planted, have sprouted, and are growing bigger and stronger with each passing day.

Spring Equinox then is a time of new life and growth. As such, it's also a time to celebrate change, which is one, if not the only, true constant in our world. The Spring Equinox is also the day when the amount of daylight and the darkness of night are equal. As a result, the symbolism of balance abounds during this festival.

Ostara's themes of balance, growth, renewal, and regeneration harmonize perfectly with the solarpunk ethos, which emphasizes a harmonious balance between technology and nature and continually seeks new, sustainable solutions to environmental and social challenges.

Ostara celebrates the triumph of day over night as the days start to grow longer, bringing the promise of warmer weather and the renewal of plant life. This triumph of the Sun is especially poignant for the solarpunk community with its focus on solar energy as a renewable and clean source of power, symbolic of hope, growth, and the power of nature.

Furthermore, Ostara's association with fertility and growth mirrors solarpunk's emphasis on the sustainable growth of resilient communities and ecosystems. It's a time of planting seeds and planning for the harvest to come, both in a literal and metaphorical sense. For solarpunks, this could translate into the commencement

56 For more details on the web of life, check out University of Illinois's online extension resources: web.extension.illinois.edu/ecosystems/teacherguide6.cfm

of community projects such as urban gardens or solar power installations, or the setting of personal goals related to sustainable living and social justice activism.

In this context, an Ostara celebration within the solarpunk community might include a tree-planting ceremony, the creation of seed bombs[57] for later dispersal, or working together to develop the community's solar power capacity. The community might share a potluck meal with locally-sourced foods, exchange ideas for new green initiatives, or simply take a moment to appreciate the Sun and its vital role in our lives and the ecosystem.

Considering Ostara's inherently solarpunk focus on balance, we can put creative intention and power into creating and fostering balance on our planet, in our society, in our specific communities and neighborhoods, and in the relationships between each of the above and nature.

One easy way to do this in groups or individually is with a spell using plant magick. Above, I briefly alluded to this idea with the suggestion of a tree-planting ceremony. But it doesn't need to be a tree. It can be anything—from a giant tree to much smaller individual potted wildflowers. With all that in mind, let's dive a little deeper into how to perform a plant magick spell.

You'll need some supplies like a pot, soil, and either seeds or a young sproutling. As you plant the seed or sprout, focus your intention on balance. It can be for balance within yourself, for the planet, for your community, for your relationship with the Earth, or for all the above.

You can also focus on the growth aspect of Spring by imbuing the planting with your intentions around the things you want to grow in your life over the next year. In the vein of solarpunk

---

57 Seed bombs are a mixture of wet soil, clay, and seeds—usually wildflower seeds that encourage pollinators. The mixture is clumped together into small balls and dried. These balls can then be thrown out into your yard or elsewhere during the winter and early spring where they'll hopefully (and usually do) germinate, take root, and grow. Nowadays. you don't have to make your own. You can easily find and buy seed bombs online made with flower seeds native to whatever region you live in.

magick, that intention could be something like the growth of your dedication to climate solutions and the sustainability movement or the growth of your antiracist consciousness and your dedication to being an active accomplice in the struggle to end white supremacy and western imperialism. You could also focus on the growth of your knowledge and application of permaculture principles and DIY solutions, or the growth and strengthening of your community and its resilience, among many other possibilities.

Beltane/May Day

Beltane is a fire festival traditionally celebrated on May 1, marking the midpoint between the Spring Equinox and the Summer Solstice in the Pagan Wheel of the Year. It's a celebration of fertility, abundance, and the blossoming vitality of Spring. It symbolizes the start of summer and the peak of spring, when life is blooming, fertile, and full of potential. These elements of growth, abundance, and vibrant life resonate powerfully within the context of solarpunk.

The solarpunk movement orients itself around a vision of a prosperous, green future that harmonizes human societies with nature. Beltane's themes of life, fertility, and abundance symbolize this solarpunk vision, echoing its focus on fostering growth—of plants and green spaces, of renewable technologies, of sustainable communities, and of the individual's connection with nature and the broader community.

The Beltane fire, traditionally lit to honor the return of the Sun and its life-giving warmth, can be seen within a solarpunk context as representing the solar energy that fuels a sustainable future. The dance around the Maypole, an activity often associated with Beltane, signifies the interconnectedness and weaving together of the diverse communities within nature, another key solarpunk value.

Moreover, Beltane is traditionally a time for action, for doing things that bring joy and foster growth. This aligns with the proactive nature of the solarpunk movement, which encourages direct action towards creating a sustainable future, whether through local food production, clean energy generation, social justice activism, or fostering resilient, sustainable communities.

A solarpunk Beltane celebration might involve community projects such as planting a communal garden, starting a renewable energy project, or organizing a fair to showcase local, sustainable crafts and technologies. It might also include communal meals made from local, seasonal produce, and shared stories and visions of a vibrant, sustainable future.

Centuries ago and more, Celtic farmers would light huge bonfires and drive their cattle between them to bring fertility to the land and health to the cattle.[58] Nowadays, at least in the particular tradition I first studied in, a form of this fire magick is still practiced. We'd light a fire, often in a small, shin-high, cast iron cauldron to help ensure the activity is as safe as possible. People, friends, family members, lovers then all took turns jumping over the fire and dropping in their insecurities and disharmony to burn and disappear to ashes in the flames. People who didn't want to or couldn't jump would either walk or roll by the fire.

The above fire magick can easily be done in groups or solitary. It can also easily be retooled specifically toward solarpunk magick. As you jump over the Beltane fire, drop into the flames disharmonies you have with your community or drop all of humanity's disharmony with nature. Watch them burn away into nothing as you visualize harmony between yourself, your community, and the Earth.

A fun one that's standard at Beltane is dancing around a Maypole full of colorful ribbons dangling down toward the ground. It's another old tradition, and a great example of both fertility magick and group dance magick. As witches dance around the Maypole, we visualize fertility coming into our lives in various forms, and we focus on weaving that fertility into our lives around particular intentions.

58 irisharchaeology.ie/2011/05/mayday-and-bealtaine

The Maypole dance can easily be transformed into solarpunk spellwork. As you and your group dance around the pole, or as you perform a solitary ecstatic dance, visualize fertility and growth for the Earth, for your relationship with the Earth, for justice in our world, and for the communities of resistance of which we're a part.

You also might consider participating in a may rally or protest. For over a hundred years, the labor movement has taken to the streets on the first day of May in order to demand a better world. While traditionally May Day isn't associated with the environmental movement, labor and climate change activism have come together more than ever in recent years. And there's little doubt that taking the streets to demand a better world is solarpunk as fuck.

Celebrating Beltane in a solarpunk context is a reaffirmation of the vitality and potential inherent in our natural world and our communities. It provides a tangible link between the fecundity[59] of nature and the abundant future that solarpunk envisions, underscoring the value of balance, interconnectedness, and sustainability.

Summer Solstice/Litha

Summer Solstice, also called Litha, is on the opposite side of the Wheel of the Year from Winter Solstice. As the longest day of the year, the Sun's strength is at its peak.

Metaphorically and mythologically, the Sun that was reborn on the Winter Solstice has grown, matured, and perhaps even become a parent. The longest day of the year means it's the day when the life-giving power of the Sun's energy is at the strongest it will be during the entire year. Flowers are blooming and the first fruits are beginning to ripen.

For this reason, Summer Solstice is a day for bonfires and feasting and celebrating the power and expansiveness of the Sun. Litha is a day to head outside with your friends, family, or coven to

---

59 Another word for fertility; the ability to produce a lot of new offspring or ideas.

soak up the Sun and show gratitude for the abundance it brings into your life.

But the longest day of the year is also the shortest night of the year. Just like the light is reborn at the Winter Solstice, on the Summer Solstice the darkness and night are reborn and begin to grow stronger. The Sun, then, is at a threshold, about to enter the period of its life cycle during which dwindling and deterioration set in.

This makes the Summer Solstice an important time of liminality. Sitting on the line separating the waxing and waning year. It's a time of transition, the onset of decline. The slide into death begins.

Sitting on the line between waxing and waning, the transition from light to darkness, means Litha also sits on the threshold fertility and harvest. The fertility of spring is turning into the harvest of late summer and autumn. Because of this, Summer Solstice has traditionally been a time of petition for a strong and healthy harvest, whether that means a harvest on the farm or in a garden, or harvesting whatever else you may want to bring into your life, your community, and movements for justice in abundance over the coming season.

In the context of solarpunk, the Sun isn't just a celestial body but a symbol of an abundant, sustainable energy source. Litha, as a celebration of the Sun at its strongest, could symbolize the potential and hope that solar energy represents. It's a reminder of our capability to harness this energy and use it to power a future that's harmonious with the natural world, echoing solarpunk's goal of creating sustainable societies that are seamlessly integrated with the ecosystems they inhabit.

Moreover, the Summer Solstice is a moment of balance, albeit a fleeting one, with the longest day matched by the shortest night. This notion of balance between light and dark resonates with the solarpunk ethos of harmonizing technology with nature, modernity with tradition, and society with individuality. It's a dance that weaves polarities into harmonious and beautiful unities, itself an alchemical and magickal act of transformation.

In a solarpunk Litha celebration, there might be a communal gathering to acknowledge and appreciate the Sun's power, perhaps by viewing the sunrise or by reflecting on the role of solar energy in our lives and our communities. It could involve the symbolic or actual use of solar panels to demonstrate the harnessing of the Sun's power. The celebration might also include discussions or workshops on renewable energy technologies, communal meals made from locally-sourced produce, and the sharing of solarpunk stories and visions.

Because flowers are in full bloom, floral activities and magickal work are usually part of the Summer Solstice. One common tradition is making a bouquet or some kind of flower-associated art to represent your petition for a strong harvest in your garden, whether that garden is growing food or community. Whatever type of harvest you choose to focus on, you can put the desired energy into your arrangement, and, once the energy feels like it's at a peak, you can toss the arrangement into the Solstice fire to activate and release the spell.

But flowers aren't the only base for Litha work. Culinary magick is also common. You could make honey cakes or rosemary bread. Bake your intentions for a healthy harvest into them, then eat your creations during your Summer Solstice celebration.

You can easily turn either of the two common Litha traditions into solarpunk magick. Tailor the intention you put into your flower arrangement toward your community rather than yourself. Focus on an abundant upcoming harvest of resilience and strength for your community, or an abundance of resources for those who are economically disadvantaged. Or, you could turn your culinary magick toward the intention of harvesting an abundance of solar power throughout the summer.

Whatever relevant traditions we engage in, celebrating Litha in a solarpunk context connects the dots between the Sun's life-giving power, our ability to harness that power for sustainable living, and the balance we aspire to strike between nature and technology. It serves as a powerful reminder of the vibrant, sustainable future that solarpunks are striving to create.

Lughnasadh/Lammas

The Sabbat positioned in the middle of Summer, equidistant from the Summer Solstice and the Autumn Equinox, is Lughnasadh, which is also called Lammas. It's traditionally celebrated on August 1 and marks the beginning of the harvest season in the Pagan Wheel of the Year. The day is named for the Irish Sun god, Lugh, and is the first of the three harvest festivals. Spring fertility and community labor are coming to fruition, and it's time to begin celebrating and giving thanks for the bountiful harvest. It's a time of gratitude for the bounty of the Earth, a celebration of the first fruits of the harvest, and a recognition of the need to store up against the leaner winter months. These themes of harvest, sustainability, and preparation align strongly with the principles of solarpunk.

The first of the three harvests is the grain harvest. Grains become a focal point in Lughnasadh celebrations through ritual sacrifices from the harvest bounty. One of the more common ways this ritual sacrifice plays out in neo-pagan celebrations is by building and burning a wickerperson, kind of like a Burning Man in terms of the main event. The pagan wickerperson is constructed using plants, grasses, grains, garden vegetables, and other natural things from the Earth.

All of the materials are used to create a statue, a symbolic representation of the dying deity archetype, which is a common theme throughout world religions.[60] In Celtic paganism, Lugh, the

---

60 Encyclopedia.com has an excellent entry on this archetype: encyclopedia.com/environment/encyclopedias-almanacs-transcripts-and-maps/dying-and-rising-gods.

dying Sun god,[61] and John Barleycorn,[62] a god of the grain, are common sacrificial myths associated with Lammas. The Egyptian deity Osiris is another commonly cited example of this archetype. Of course, in this day and age, Christianity's Jesus is one of the most well known examples of the dying Sun god archetype.

A wicker basket is set on its end and is used as the base of the statue, its torso. During the ritual, participants place their own personal grain sacrifice into the basket to be burned and sacrificed along with wickerperson. Before placing the grain in the basket, each participant charges their grain with gratitude for the bounty in their lives, and with the intention of releasing something in their lives that no longer serves them.

Then, the wickerperson is burned, and the witches dance around the fire, celebrating and feasting on the bounty of the Sun and Earth.

This theme of sacrifice can also be infused with the spirit of radical hope and resistance, turning the ritual burning of the wickerperson into a work of solarpunk magick. One option is to visualize the fossil fuel industry being sacrificed and burning away into the dustbin of history to make way for a sustainable future based on clean and renewable energy sources. Another option is that you can charge your grain with your intention for what you're going to sacrifice in order to help make that better, future world a present day reality.

That sacrifice can take many forms. It can be a sacrifice of time and effort, organizing resources, or monetary and other resources valuable to the movement. It could also be the sacrifice of putting your body and freedom on the line by engaging in civil disobedience. Regardless of your comfort level when it comes to radical political

---

61 You can start learning more about Lugh with the *World History Encyclopedia*: worldhistory.org/Lugh.
62 More on John Barleycorn can be found at in this primer at *Learn Religions*: learnreligions.com/the-legend-of-john-barleycorn-2562157.

engagement, there are plenty of ways to focus your sacrifice so it becomes solarpunk magick.

Lughnasadh is also the first Sabbat situated firmly within the waning year, the time of decline. On this day, you can visualize the decline of fossil fuel use and companies, the decline of corruption and capitalism, or the decline of fascism and white supremacy. There are a lot of options. Visualize what you want to decline in your life or in our world as you place your grain into the wickerperson to be burned in the sacrificial fire.

In solarpunk, there's also a strong focus on sustainable living, which includes growing one's own food, supporting local agriculture, and being mindful of the resources we consume. Lammas as a celebration of the harvest resonates with these concepts. It's an opportunity to appreciate the abundance provided by nature and to reinforce the importance of sustainable, regenerative practices in agriculture.

Moreover, Lammas carries with it the awareness of the cyclical nature of the seasons, of times of plenty and of scarcity, reminding us of the necessity of planning and preparedness. This reminder parallels the solarpunk emphasis on building resilient communities that can withstand and adapt to challenges, whether they are environmental, social, or economic.

In the context of a solarpunk Lammas celebration, you might find community gatherings centered around the harvest. This could involve communal meals prepared with locally-sourced produce, sharing the fruits of community gardens, or organizing food preservation workshops to demonstrate ways of storing the summer's bounty for the colder months.

Activities could also include discussions or workshops on permaculture, sustainable farming, and the importance of local food systems. In a more symbolic sense, there might be the telling of stories or shared reflections on the themes of abundance, sustainability, and community resilience.

Celebrating Lammas within the solarpunk movement serves as a reminder of our connection to the Earth and the cycles of nature. It reinforces the importance of sustainability, community resilience, and the value of local, regenerative agricultural practices. In essence, it's a celebration of the harvest that both honors the abundance of the Earth and encourages mindful stewardship of its resources, mirroring the solarpunk vision of a harmonious, sustainable future.

Autumn Equinox/Mabon

Fall Equinox is the polar opposite of Spring Equinox. The Equinoxes are the two days of the year when the amount of daylight and darkness are equal. Autumn is a time of balance then, just like spring. Mythologically, it's the last day in which the power of the archetype of light is stronger than that of the archetype of darkness.

The next day will be shorter than the night time, as the archetype of darkness—often portrayed as a ruler of the underworld—ascends in power in contrast to the Sun's decline and steady movement toward death. Autumn Equinox invites us to recognize the onset of darkness and the time of quiet reflection on the lessons we accumulated during the more active part of our lives.

Mabon[63] is also the second of the three harvest festivals, the fruit harvest. In line with the theme of darkness, quiet reflection, and the waning year, this Equinox is a time of rest after the hard work of harvesting that which will nourish and sustain the family and community through the rest of autumn and the winter season. Those three main themes—balance, harvest, and the rising power of the dark time of year—are the basis of magickal work done at Mabon festivals. As a time of balance, at Mabon, witches often do work around creating balance in their own lives. On the theme of harvest, work done during Mabon doesn't look entirely different

63 Mabon is a Welsh god who is the son of the Earth goddess and is referred to as the Child of Light. As far as can be seen from existing evidence, Fall Equinox was a particularly important day for ancient Celtic paganism. The earliest known association between the god Mabon and the Fall Equinox only goes back to the 1970s: goddessandgreenman.co.uk/mabon.

from that done at Lammas. While there's not another wickerperson, magickal work commonly focuses on gratitude and releasing—or sacrificing—what no longer serve us.

In solarpunk, there's a significant emphasis on creating balanced, sustainable societies that respect and work with nature. Mabon, as a time of equilibrium, resonates with this concept. The equal length of day and night symbolizes the balance between the use of technology and the preservation of nature, the balance between individual needs and communal responsibilities, and the balance between sustainable growth and resource conservation. As a solarpunk witch, you could perform magick around creating balance between yourself, your habits, and nature, thereby fostering a more harmonious relationship with the Earth and your local ecosystem. You could do similar work pertaining to balance within your community, or within our society and world in general.

Furthermore, Mabon is a time of giving thanks for the Earth's bounty, of harvesting and preserving the abundance for the winter ahead. This idea of harvest links to solarpunk's emphasis on sustainable living, permaculture, and community resilience. It's a time to acknowledge the bounty that nature provides and to ensure it's used and preserved responsibly.

A solarpunk celebration of Mabon might involve communal meals prepared with the final harvest of the season, using locally sourced, seasonal foods. The celebration could also include discussions on sustainability, workshops on permaculture design, or storytelling that centers on themes of balance and gratitude. As a solarpunk witch, you might focus on the sacrifices people in the community have made over the past year in service of building more resilient communities, fighting for equality and an end to white supremacy, working for climate solutions, etc. You can lean into the onset of the dark time of the year and reflect on the lessons that can be learned from those sacrifices and how they can be applied to your life and community in a way that serves the aspiration of building a better world. Then, find a way to show gratitude to them through your ritual work and activities.

There might be practical demonstrations of sustainability and resource conservation, such as workshops on food preservation, energy conservation, or winterizing homes. The equinox could also be a time to plan community projects for the coming winter or to share progress and learnings from the growing season.

In short, celebrating Mabon in a solarpunk context connects the community to the cycle of the seasons and the balance in nature. It is a time to appreciate the bounty of the Earth, to share and conserve resources, and to strengthen community bonds. As such, Mabon beautifully encapsulates the solarpunk vision of a sustainable, resilient, and balanced society.

Samhain

Samhain is the Feast of the Dead and the Celtic New Year. It takes place from October 31 through November 1, and is the root of both the Christian All Saints' Day and the modern holiday favorite, Halloween.[64] In many ways it's also similar to the Day of the Dead which—also celebrated on November 1—is recognized by many Latinx folks around the world. Like the Day of the Dead, Samhain is a day on which we honor the ancestors who've come and gone before us, on whose shoulders we sit or stand as we move into the future armed with the radical hope of generational struggle.

This third and final harvest festival is firmly situated within the dark and waning time of the year. Samhain is a time of death. Mythologically, it's the time of year when we celebrate the Sun's death and descent into the Underworld, where it resides until the time of rebirth comes once again at Yule. That makes this a time to celebrate the harvest of life and of souls. Samhain is a time to reflect on the lessons we can learn from our ancestors and from the

---

64 The Library of Congress blog has a great article about Samhain as a predecessor of All Saints' Day and Halloween: blogs.loc.gov/headlinesandheroes/2021/10/the-origins-of-halloween-traditions.

past, whether it's our individual past, our family past, or a larger collective past.

A common part of Samhain rituals then, is a candle ceremony for the ancestors. Over the years, I've been to numerous Samhain rituals with different groups from varying traditions. Every single one of them has included this aspect.

To perform the ceremony, you need a black candle (white is also commonly used), a way to light the candles, and a cauldron. It's also a good idea to have thin cardboard or thick parchment discs with a small X cut into the center. You can slip your candle into the hole, and the disc will help protect your hand from dripping hot wax during the ceremony. Since it's usually cold at this time of year and Samhain ceremonies are usually performed indoors, this disc protects the carpet, wood, linoleum, or whatever flooring you're on during the ceremony. If you're performing this ritual by yourself or with a very small group of people, you can remove or modify the spiral dance portion of the ceremony.

You'll essentially perform the basic solarpunk ritual, and the ceremony for the ancestors will be the main activity and magickal work performed. The candle ceremony starts by passing out candles and discs to each participant. Whoever is going to light their candle first does so, using the central altar candle, which will already be lit at this point in the ritual. That person then holds their candle for the next person to use to light their own, and so on around the ritual circle, until everyone's candle is lit with a burning flame.

Once all the candles are lit, one participant begins and leads the spiral dance. Everyone follows the guide, moving round and round, further inward forming a spiral. As you move around the circle you look directly at each person as you pass by them. You see the ancestors and their wisdom reflected in the eyes of each and every person. Eventually, the person in front reaches the center of the spiral and begins weaving their way back outward. Once each participant reaches the outer end of the spiral, they remove the paper disc and safely place their candle in the cauldron. Those candles are then used to spark the central ceremonial fire in honor of the ancestors.

To move a Samhain ritual into solarpunk territory, you can further focus your ceremony on the ancestors of the environmental movement and other movements for justice. You can also reflect on past movements themselves. Consider the lessons and wisdom they have to teach us going forward in the struggle to build a better and more utopian world.

From a solarpunk perspective, Samhain holds a unique symbolism that aligns with its principles of resilience, sustainability, and community. Samhain's association with the end of the harvest season resonates with solarpunk's emphasis on sustainability and cyclical patterns of nature. It signifies the end of one cycle and the preparation for the next, a time to reflect on the lessons learned from the past growing season and plan for the future. It's a reminder of the need to adapt and prepare for the challenges of the coming winter months, which echoes solarpunk's focus on resilience and adaptability in the face of environmental and societal changes.

Moreover, the connection of Samhain to ancestors and the spirit world can function in solarpunk as a metaphor for historical and generational wisdom. This could involve valuing and learning from past societies that lived more sustainably or acknowledging our responsibility to future generations. In a broader sense, a solarpunk Samhain highlights the interconnectedness of all beings, not just in the physical realm but across time, promoting a sense of continuity and collective responsibility.

In addition, or instead of a spiral dance, a solarpunk Samhain celebration might include reflecting on the past year's successes and challenges in sustainable living and community projects. This could be done through storytelling, sharing experiences, or quiet contemplation. The celebration could also honor those who have pioneered sustainable practices and green technologies, acknowledging them as ancestors of the solarpunk movement.

Moreover, the Samhain celebration could involve preparing for the winter season in a sustainable and community-oriented way, such as winterizing community gardens, organizing clothes or food drives, or sharing methods for conserving energy during the colder months.

Samhain in the context of solarpunk is about acknowledging cycles—of the Earth, of life and death, and of societal progression. It's a time for reflection and learning, for honoring the wisdom of the past, and preparing for the future. It reminds us of our place in the great cycle of life, our interconnectedness with all beings, and our responsibility to strive for a sustainable and equitable future.

LUNARPUNK: CELEBRATING ESBATS

As we delve into the cycle of Esbats, we come to another critical component of modern witchcraft practices. Rooted deeply in mythology and ritual, Esbats are gatherings or solitary observances that follow the lunar cycle, providing a powerful conduit for harnessing the Moon's energy and exploring the depths of spiritual growth and transformation.

Esbats are typically celebrated during the full Moon when the Moon's energy is at its peak, though they are sometimes also celebrated during the new Moon. Unlike Sabbats, which are primarily solar and tied to the Earth's seasonal cycle, Esbats are tied to the lunar cycle and are typically observed twelve to thirteen times a year. They offer a more frequent opportunity for Craft practitioners to come together or reflect individually, allowing for a steady rhythm of spiritual work within the larger Wheel of the Year.

The Esbat-associated mythology is varied and rich. Many traditions associate the full Moon with the goddess in her full aspect—the Mother—symbolizing fulfillment, fruition, and abundance. The new Moon, on the other hand, often aligns with the Crone aspect of the goddess, representing wisdom, transformation, and the potential for new beginnings. This cyclical view of the

Moon's phases resonates with the cyclical view of life, death, and rebirth that is fundamental to many pagan and witchcraft traditions. Keep in mind that many cultures attribute male gender to Moon deities, but there's no right or wrong way to conceive of such beings.[65]

The Esbat ritual practices are as diverse as the practitioners themselves, which should come as no surprise. Some may hold elaborate ceremonies involving casting a circle, calling the quarters, invoking deities, spellwork, divination, or sharing a ritual meal. Others tend to prefer a simpler observance, such as Moon bathing, meditating, journaling, or charging their tools in the moonlight. The core intent, however, remains the same: to honor the lunar cycle, tap into the Moon's energy, and use this time for spiritual growth, transformation, or magickal work.

In modern witchcraft, Esbats play an essential role in providing regular opportunities for practitioners to connect with lunar energies and their personal spirituality. These rituals offer a space for introspection, transformation, and the strengthening of witchcraft skills, whether that's through spellwork, divination, or simply attuning one's self to the natural rhythms of the Moon. They are a fundamental pillar of witchcraft practice, a monthly reminder of our intimate connection to the Moon, and our place within the larger, ever-turning wheel of life. But how do Esbats fit in with the practice of solarpunk witchcraft?

In solarpunk, the celebration of Esbats aligns beautifully with the movement's foundational principles of interconnectedness, harmony, and a cyclic understanding of time. Recognizing the Esbats serves as a regular reminder of our relationship with the natural world, and specifically the rhythms and cycles of the Moon. This consistent observance encourages mindfulness of the celestial sphere's influence on our daily lives and environment, thereby nurturing a deeper connection to the world around us.

65 Personally, when I use deities or archetypes, I generally prefer nonbinary versions, reflecting my own identity. Though there are still times when I do use gendered archetypes.

Solarpunk primarily focuses on the creation of a future where humanity and nature exist in symbiosis, with renewable and sustainable technology serving as the bridge between the two. The Moon, being our closest celestial neighbor, and a governing force over many natural cycles on Earth, plays a crucial role in this vision. The lunar cycle is a stark symbol of cyclicity and change—the waning and waxing, the ebb and flow, the perpetual dance of growth and retreat that shapes so many aspects of our world.

For example, the Moon's phases influence the tides, an interaction of celestial and earthly forces that exemplifies the kind of harmony and interplay solarpunk strives to emulate in human society. Furthermore, the Moon's cycles have been used in traditional agriculture to determine the best times for planting and harvesting, a practice that aligns well with solarpunk's emphasis on permaculture and sustainable farming techniques.

In terms of ritual observance, a solarpunk Esbat might be more focused on community-building and practical sustainability efforts. These might include moonlit gatherings to discuss community projects, sharing knowledge about local ecology, or even nocturnal gardening by moonlight. Just as the Moon gently illuminates the night, these gatherings can serve to enlighten and inspire, fostering a sense of communal solidarity and shared purpose.

Moreover, the introspective and transformative aspects of the Esbats resonate with solarpunk's emphasis on personal and societal transformation. The new Moon, a time of potential and beginnings, might be seen as an opportunity to brainstorm new ideas for sustainable technologies or community initiatives. The full Moon, a time of fruition and completion, could be a time to celebrate the progress of ongoing projects or to simply appreciate the beauty of a world where technology and nature coexist peacefully.

Ultimately, the Esbats in a solarpunk context embody the movement's aim to harmonize our technological existence with the natural world's cycles. By observing these lunar celebrations, solarpunks reinforce their commitment to a sustainable future, highlighting the cyclical nature of time, the importance of community, and the continual interplay between humanity, technology, and the natural world. Whether or not you choose to couch those activities with some kind of Esbat variation of the basic ritual for solarpunk witches (see Chapter Four) is entirely up to you. For those who want a ritual observance, I've outlined a basic Esbat ritual for solarpunk witches below, which leans into the aesthetic and symbolism of the solarpunk subgenre, lunarpunk.[66] (See the appendix for more on lunarpunk.)

As a final note before we dive into the ritual: each full Moon has its own set of correspondences you can incorporate into each monthly Esbat, if you want to. Each Moon generally has a name with symbolic meaning such as the blood Moon or harvest Moon. I don't tend to do this when I perform Esbat rituals, keeping it a bit more simple. For that reason, the following ritual doesn't lean heavily into such correspondences. But feel free to explore, including your findings in your own versions of the ritual below.

Preparation

Begin by getting yourself into a ritual state of mind. If you take any kind of ritual bath prior to rituals, now is the time to do so. Then perform the sacred grove meditation on page 65 to relax the body and mind.

Prepare your ritual space, preferably outdoors under the open sky, and ideally where you can see the Moon. Mark your circle with glow-in-the-dark pebbles or painted stones, creating a radiant, luminescent boundary that captures the essence of moonlight. In a pinch, you can generally find glow sticks at a dollar store or similar places, though I'd generally recommend staying away from the use of plastics as much as possible.

---

66 Lunarpunk is a subgenre of solarpunk. The themes of sustainability, harmony with nature, social justice, and resilient and adaptable communities resonate throughout lunarpunk, the same as solarpunk. The main difference between the two is the literary and artistic aesthetic. While solarpunk is bright and sunny and rooted in art nouveau, lunarpunk is dark and gothic and spiritual: it leans into bioluminescence and a color palette of purple, silver, black, and the like.

Arrange your altar in the center of the circle, using a black cloth adorned with silver or glowing symbols as your base. On your altar, place a white or silver candle to represent the moon, as well as an incense of jasmine or sandalwood, both of which are associated with the Moon and its energy. Of course, you can use whatever incense you want, especially if (for whatever reason) you aren't partial to the smell of jasmine or sandalwood.

Include moon-charged crystals such as selenite or moonstone, a chalice of water charged under the moon, and a bowl of salt or soil, which combined with the candles and incense represent the four elements. You may also want to add symbols of Moon deity archetypes and a handheld mirror.

Wear clothing that feels comfortable and fitting for the occasion. Dark, flowing clothes adorned with glowing accessories, or even bioluminescent jewelry if available, would suit the lunarpunk aesthetic of this ritual perfectly.

Casting the Circle

Begin by standing at the edge of your circle, facing East. With your dominant hand, point your athame (or index and middle finder), and imagine a beam of luminescent energy flowing from your fingertips. Slowly moving deosil, or clockwise, use that energy to draw a protective boundary along the perimeter of your circle. As you move along the circle, see the energy forming, infusing your circle, deepening the glow of your boundary rocks. When you return to your starting place in the East, you can use your athame to tie a knot of light and seal the circle. If you want to recite a poem or chant as you cast the circle, you can try something along the lines of this:

By the powers of Earth, Air, Fire, and Water,
By the radiance of the Moon
I cast this circle as a place between worlds
And seal it while we observe this rite.

Calling the Quarters

Stand facing East and say: "I call upon the East, the breath of dawn and the whisper of wind. Illuminate us with the knowledge of the Air."

Turn South and say: "I call upon the South, the warmth of daylight and the spark of life. Illuminate us with the passion of Fire."

Face West and say: "I call upon the West, the embrace of twilight and the flow of rivers. Illuminate us with the intuition of Water."

Lastly, turn to the North and say: "I call upon the North, the cloak of night and the wisdom of stone. Illuminate us with the grounding of the Earth."

After you call each quarter, you may wish to use your wand to draw a symbol of power such as a pentagram, or a symbol that represents the element of that quarter.

Invocation of the Moon

Return to your altar, gaze at the Moon or your white candle, and say:

Celestial Luminary, resplendent orb of night,
guide us through shadowed valleys with your radiant, silver
light.
Be our beacon, our compass, our stalwart guide
as we traverse the unseen pathways where mysteries hide.
Bathe our hearts in your soothing glow,
awaken our minds to the wisdom you bestow.
Engulf our souls in your tranquil tide,
in your gentle illumination, let us confide.

Magickal Work

This is the time for personal spellwork, meditation, or divination. You can use any of the ideas tossed around above or come up with your own sustainability and social justice oriented magickal work to do.

Fellowship

Now that you've completed the magickal work portion of the ritual, it's time to break bread. Pour a small glass of libation, and take a small piece of bread, cake, or whatever food you have available, and place them on the altar as an offering to the moon, to your archetypes, as a symbolic offering to those in need. Then take some time to relax and enjoy food and drink (especially if you're doing a group ritual). You can also use this time to share eco-solutions, new tech ideas, or community projects that align with solarpunk principles.

Grounding

When your ritual workings are complete, hold the chalice of moon-charged water in your hands. Visualize the glowing energy of the Moon flowing into the water, and as you drink, imagine that energy filling and grounding you. If you'd like, you can say a few words as you ground, such as:

Feet rooted in the pulsing Earth, to the core our spirits connect,

In the grounding depth, we find rebirth, in warm embrace our hearts reflect.

Beneath us lies the ancient soil, a testament to time's grand play,

Within its depths, our worries coil, to be absorbed and swept away.

Mighty trees and humble grass, alike in stature, strength, and grace,

Solarpunk's vision clear as glass, in each blade, each leaf, we trace.

Echoes of the moon's soft glow, mirrored in the life below,
In the grounding depth, we come to know the cycle of life's ebb and flow.

Opening the Circle

When you're ready, thank the Moon and the elemental forces for their presence, starting with the North and moving counterclockwise. As you thank each direction, visualize the luminescent boundary fading, but the energy staying with you. Conclude the ritual with the words: "The circle is open, but unbroken."

End the ritual by blowing out your candle. Spend some time basking in the moonlight, enjoying the peaceful ambience of the bioluminescent night, and grounding yourself with a light snack. Remember to leave the area as undisturbed as possible, keeping in line with the solarpunk ethos of respecting and preserving nature.

•　　　•　　　•

Sabbats and Esbats are easily adapted to the framework of solarpunk witchcraft by integrating traditional pagan celebrations with the solarpunk ethos of sustainability, community, and harmony with nature. Sabbats, rooted in the solar calendar, reflect the cyclical nature of the seasons and the Sun's journey, offering opportunities for solarpunks to engage in rituals that align with ecological cycles and sustainable living. Esbats, on the other hand, are tied to the lunar cycle and provide a rhythm for more frequent spiritual work, emphasizing the interconnectedness of all beings and the influence of celestial bodies on the Earth. Through these celebrations, solarpunk witches aim to foster a deep connection with the natural world, drawing on the symbolism and energy of Sabbats and Esbats to reinforce our commitment to creating a harmonious and sustainable future.

Chapter Six: Sun Magick for Solarpunk Witches

*T*n this next chapter, we'll dig into meditations, magick, and correspondences solarpunk witches use that focus on the Sun and its energy as a base of spiritual and magickal power. These are Sun-based versions of the kinds of practices witches do in general, like meditations, altar composition, oil and incense blend recipes, and other such things. The examples below can all weave into your general solarpunk spirituality and Craft practice.

SUN MEDITATIONS

There are so many ways to meditate. You can sit quietly and empty your mind, you can use a focal point. You can meditate with the purpose of relaxing your physical body. You can do active and moving meditations, meditations with eyes closed and with eyes open (focusing on awareness), meditations that focus on different methods of breathing, and many more. Below are five examples of meditations that focus on the Sun, its energy, and our relationship with it.

Sun Meditation #1: Breathing in the Sun

The Sun's energy is life force. It's a necessary component for the existence of life on Earth. As such, the Sun is a symbol of vitality, virility, passion, fire, energy, and power.

These associations exist in a range of spiritual practices around the world. In Hatha Yoga, for example, the Sun is life force and solar energy, also called prana, that we can take into us through exposure and breathing, promoting health and increasing our energy. Breathing in early morning prana has been incorporated into many neo-pagan traditions. Personally, I first learned about breathing in the Sun not through yoga, but through a Druidic Craft tradition I was a coven member of in my early twenties.

A very simple Sun meditation you can practice daily is to simply go outside and stand or sit in the Sun, close your eyes, take deep breaths, and relax. While you're doing so, you can keep your mind as clear and relaxed as possible, or you can use a particular example of Sun symbolism as a focal point. You can simply sit quietly with a silent mind, feeling and basking in the Sun, or you can contemplate the Sun and its meaning for your life.

You don't have to choose one example of the above and stick with it, though you certainly can if that works best for you. But you can also switch it up among all the listed varieties from time-to-time or create your own variations to keep your meditations fresh and meaningful.

As you breathe, feel the warm energy of the Sun filing your lungs. Feel it electrify you as your breath and the Sun's power work their way into your bloodstream and are distributed throughout your body. As you continue breathing, the light of the Sun floods and fills your inner being. It's cozy, soft, warm, and relaxing, even while it's refreshing, invigorating, and inspirational. Sit in the light and energy of the Sun, breathing into your body for as long as you need to.

Sun Meditation #2: Relaxation & Safe Space

Using meditation to relax the body and mind in preparation for ritual and magickal work is a basic practice. The following is based on a meditation I learned from a friend when I was in high school and first learning about witchcraft. I've since adapted it to use the Sun as the meditation's central focus and imagery.

To begin, sit in a quiet and comfortable place. Take three slow, deep, conscious and active breaths in through your nose and out through your mouth. As you breathe in, say to yourself, "Relax." As you breathe out, say to yourself, "Relax now." Feel the tension oozing out of your body, leaking out of your pores. As you continue breathing, with each inhale, visualize the warm and cleansing light of the Sun being carried on your breath and filling your body. As you breathe out, see all the stress and worry, the tension and anxiety of the day, slip away, leaving you and your body and being carried away and evaporating into nothing with each exhale.

Once you feel completely relaxed, you notice that the powerful and electrifying light of the Sun has completely filled your body. With your next breath, that light explodes out of the crown of your head, bursting forth and falling around you like a fountain of peace and safety.

As the light continues to fill you and pour out of you, it surrounds you in a big ball of Sunlight. See that ball of fire form and take shape around you. Touch its inner boundary and feel the searing heat and impenetrable power of the Sun. This sphere of solar power surrounds and protects you. It shields you, and the flames devour negative energy, hexes, and other powers that might seek to harm you and drag you down.

You feel warm. You feel relaxed. You feel at peace. You feel balanced. You feel safe. Nothing can harm you while you're within the protected space of your Sun sphere. Do this meditation as often as you feel the need.

Sun Meditation #3: Daily Solar Phases

The following meditation focuses on the Sun's daily phases and the spiritual associations of each phase. You can do this meditation regularly to help foster a closer and more harmonious relationship with the Sun and its spiritual energy. If it's helpful, you can read the meditation into a voice recording app on your phone or computer, and then play it back as a realtime guide while doing the meditation.

Pick a quiet, comfortable spot to sit. Preferably somewhere you know you won't be interrupted. Sit in whatever manner is most comfortable for you. You can also lay down instead if you prefer.

Next, close your eyes and begin taking long, slow, deep breaths. Breathe in through your nose while saying to yourself, "Relax." Hold the breath for a three count, then slowly release a long exhale through your mouth while saying, "Relax now" to yourself. Again, hold the breath at the end of exhale for a count of three before beginning your next deep inhale.

Take a few good, conscious breaths in this manner, relaxing your body and mind before delving into the meditation. When you're ready, continue.

As you keep breathing and relaxing, begin to see yourself in the dark, early morning hours before the Sun has risen on the eastern horizon. You're out in nature, in a place where you have a full view of the sky from horizon to horizon. You might see yourself thousands of feet up on a tall mountain peak. Perhaps you're in the middle of a great open plain—grasslands with an unobstructed view as far as you can see. You might even imagine yourself floating on giant ocean swells. It can be any setting that satisfies two conditions: a view of the Sun's entire path across the sky and a place that's relaxing for you.

You continue breathing steadily, and, in your mind, you take a seat and look around. The sky's still dark, but it begins to lighten, visibility improves, and the scene comes into focus as the Sun pokes its first rays above the distant horizon. As the Sun rises into a fresh, morning bluebird sky, you can feel warm rays caress your skin as a light wind gently tussles your hair. This is a powerful time of new beginnings. The creative force of the morning Sun fills you, encourages you, and gives you vitality and confidence.

As you watch the morning Sun, your mind is filled with new ideas, goals, and inspirations that excite you and fill you with hope for tomorrow. Latch onto one of these ideas and let it sit in your mind. Think about it and see it clearly. Continue the meditation by allowing new ideas, goals, and inspirations to arise until you feel ready to move on.

Continue breathing. Continue relaxing. Feel the tension leaking from your muscles and joints as you slip deeper into comfort and peace. Notice details about the scenery as the Sun moves its way up into the center of the sky, directly above you.

It's now midday, at time of action and progress, a time of moving from idea and inspiration to concrete reality. As you breathe, you think about the ways you can move the ideas and inspirations and goals you had in the morning toward actionable tasks and projects to make those ideas reality. Take some time to focus on one of these projects. Then look around and enjoy the peaceful, calming view. Soak up the fiery power of the midday Sun, the energy of action and forward momentum.

When you're ready to move on, you notice that the Sun has crept down toward the western horizon. The sky is exploding in a splattering of oranges, reds, and purples as the Sun sets for the evening. As you continue breathing, thoughts of fruition and completion surface. You see the ideas that became projects now become whole and complete.

Finally, your mind turns to the things you want to let go of in your life—thoughts and visions of things no longer serving to you. You make the conscious choice to release each one of them. See them moving out of your mind and floating up into the air. Those things that no longer serve you travel toward the West and set with the Sun, disappearing behind the horizon and from your life.

Say some words of gratitude. Continue breathing until you feel ready to open your eyes and end the meditation.

Sun Meditation #4: The Fire Within

The Sun is a great ball of fire navigating the Milky Way. In combination with other factors, it makes life on our planet possible. The following meditation explores fire in both this creative and life giving role, as well as in its destructive force and capacity. It can be used regularly to help build a connection with the power and energies of fire and the Sun. As a consistent practice, this meditation has been helpful for my own anger management purposes.

Close your eyes and take your three long, deep, relaxing breaths. Then, as you continue breathing, see a flame forming in your mind's eye. It starts as a single, small flame, like that produced by a candle.

The flame is engulfed in a comforting blanket of darkness, a pitch black ocean of nothing that surrounds the flame and absorbs everything else around it.

You can't help but wonder if the universe has ceased to exist. Perhaps, just maybe, it never really existed in the first place. Maybe the safety and loving silence of the darkness is all there's ever been.

Continue breathing. Notice the flame grow in size to that of a small campfire. Feel the flame's heat warm you as it licks your skin. Feel the light charge you as it grows in the darkness and fills your being.

Your body begins buzzing with the power of life as the light and heat of the fire continue to grow. Feel your being vibrating with the electro-static pulse of the Sun's heart. Inspiration flows through you. Creativity spills out from within you. Life bursts forth and the campfire explodes into a raging bonfire.

Continue breathing and see ancestors—both human and animal—congregating around the bonfire in a magickal dance celebrating life. Swept up in the joy and passion pouring forth from the fire, you join the ecstatic dance and lose yourself in the magick of movement.

As you dance, your body becomes one with the flames. You move as the flames move, flickering and undulating with the power of creation.

Breathing and dancing, the bonfire now grows into a giant conflagration, a raging wildfire capable of immense destruction.

Reflecting the growth of the flame, your fire dance becomes more ecstatic and erratic as the heat and static increase. The air cracks with sparks. Lightning bolts streak across the lingering darkness, lighting the outer world as they flash into being.

Now the flame burns your skin.

The pain is intense.

Passionate fury wells up within you as your skin bakes and burns in the radiant power of the ancient Sun.

Frustration and anger bubble up like lava spilling onto soil.

Breathe deeply.

Feel the pain.

Feel the righteous anger.

Recognize it and its value. Learn the lessons it has to teach you.

Allow it to exist within you.

But breathe deeply. Breathe through it.

And then breathe past it.

Release it.

Allow it to be absorbed by the loving arms of the Earth.

Feel yourself relax, calm. Feel the peace of the flame restored as it recedes back down to a single, but still significant and meaningful, flame. The light of life. The power of death.

Fire.

The Sun.

Sit and continue breathing until you feel ready to open your eyes. If you feel the need, place your feet and hands on the ground to discharge any excess energy back into the Earth.

Sun Meditation #5: Moving Sun Meditation

The final Sun meditation we'll go over here is a moving meditation.[67] It's quite simple. At its most basic, all you need to do is go for a stroll on a sunny day. Remember to keep your eyes open, of course, unlike most other kinds of meditations. You don't want to run into other people, or poles or trees or cars.

---

67 This type of meditation is usually called a "walking meditation." I prefer using the term "moving meditation," which is more inclusive of people who don't walk and rather use other forms of mobility.

Use a compass, the position of the Sun in the sky, or another method of your choosing to determine which directions are East and West. Mimicking the Sun, travel from East to West as you move along on your stroll.

Move slowly, but steadily and consciously, along your chosen path. Feel the warm Sun on your skin. Feel the fire, the Sun's passion, the creative impulse. Feel your confidence grow as the Sun's rays engulf you. Notice the way its light plays with the ecosystem around you. Explore the liminal spaces created by the relationship between the light and shadow.

Depending on how long your stroll lasts, notice the Sun's movement in the sky above you. Where does it sit now compared to when you started? Is the ambient temperature around you warmer or cooler as a result? Or has no change occurred? Notice these things and get to know the Sun better as you build a relationship with this ancient life force.

SUN CORRESPONDENCES

Many witches perform certain spells at particular times of day, depending on the kind of work they're doing. Below is a table with information on how to use the daily phases of the Sun to plan out different types of spellwork. While not necessary for a spell to be effective, using correspondences such as this is one way to put more time, thought, focus, and intention into your spellwork.

Table 1 - Phases of the Sun

Daily Sun Phases	Magickal Correspondences
Sunrise/Dawn	Renewal, resurrection, rebirth, new beginnings Change Cleansing Inspiration and creativity Awakening Revealing Shedding light on what was hidden
Morning	Growth Expansion of ideas and identity Gaining strength Seeking harmony Courage Self-confidence Planning Working and building Prosperity or abundance
Midday	Peak energy Strength Power Vitality Health Learning and acquiring
Afternoon	Communication Tying up loose ends Clarity Exploration Knowledge and wisdom

Sunset/Dusk	Releasing
	Relaxing
	Letting go of problems, stress, depression, anxiety, and confusion
	Reflection
	Decline
	Death
	Covering or keeping secrets
	Completion, cycle ending

Herbs Associated with the Sun

Herbs are used by witches for a wide variety of purposes. We blend them into charms, potions, oils, teas, salves, ointments, incense blends, and, of course, depending on the herb, they're great for cooking too.

For herbal correspondences, I generally use a book like *Cunningham's Encyclopedia of Magical Herbs*.[68] I like that source in particular because it includes a list of which are unsafe to ingest if you have particular health issues, an important consideration if you're doing culinary magick or making magickal oils. You can use the same book or a similar resource[69] to see what other magickal associations each of these herbs have, which is helpful in composing spells and other magickal rituals.

For example, saffron corresponds both to the Sun and to the element of fire. Its magickal properties include but aren't necessarily limited to healing, strength, love and lust, and enhancing psychic powers. Below, then, is a comprehensive, though incomplete, table of magickal herbs associated with the Sun that I commonly use in my practice.

---

68 An additional and free resource for herb correspondences is *The Wiccan Lady's* online Herbal Grimoire: thewiccanlady.co.uk/herbal-grimoire.

69 Be sure to keep in mind that not all sources will attribute the exact same associations to the same plants. For example, some sources such as *The Wiccan Lady* website, (thewiccanlady.co.uk/herbal-grimoire) list rue as a solar herb, while others, like the *Encyclopedia of Magical Herbs*, list rue as corresponding to the planet Mars. It's worth pointing out that, generally speaking, the Sun and Mars are often associated with a number of similar characteristics, such as being active and driven.

Table 2 - Herbs Associated with the Sun

Chamomile	This sunny little flower is associated with the Sun not only for its bright yellow centers but also for its calming, yet uplifting energy. Chamomile carries the gentle warmth of the Sun, symbolizing healing, relaxation, and peace. As a solarpunk witch, you might use chamomile in spells for emotional balance, stress relief, or spiritual enlightenment, or brew a cup of chamomile tea for its magickally calming effects.
Chrysan-themum	Revered in many cultures for its vibrant blooms that coincide with the fall sun, chrysanthemum is a symbol of the Sun's power, even as it wanes. This plant can be used in spells for longevity, protection, and rejuvenation. As a solarpunk witch, you might use chrysanthemum to connect with the endurance of the Sun, even in times of environmental adversity.
Cinnamon	Known for its warming properties and spicy aroma, cinnamon embodies the heat of the Sun. It's often used for spells of attraction, protection, and prosperity. As a solarpunk witch, you might use cinnamon to bring about change, symbolizing the transformative power of the Sun and a renewable, sustainable future.
Juniper	This evergreen plant thrives under the sun, symbolizing endurance and protection. Juniper berries can be used for protection spells or to ward off negative energy. As a solarpunk witch, juniper can symbolize the resilience of nature against adversity, echoing the sun's persistent rise every day.

Marigold	This bright flower is often used in celebrations of the Sun. Marigold embodies positive Sun energy, often used in spells for success, positivity, and growth. As a solarpunk witch, you can use marigold to infuse your actions with positivity and optimism, key aspects of solarpunk ideology.
Orange	Vibrantly colored and filled with life-giving juice, oranges are symbolic of the Sun's nurturing and revitalizing energy. Use oranges in spells for abundance, joy, and health. As a solarpunk witch, consider the orange as a symbol of a bountiful, sustainable future, where resources are managed equitably.
Sunflower	Sunflowers are famous for their heliotropism, meaning they follow the Sun, literally turning to face it throughout each day as the Sun travels across the sky. Sunflowers symbolize loyalty, adoration, and the nourishing power of the Sun. As a solarpunk witch, you can use sunflowers in rituals aimed at seeking truth and light, and promoting solar power and other renewable energy sources.

Solar Incense Blends

To create solarpunk incense blends, you can blend any of the herbs listed above. You can buy the herbs already dried, of course. But it's even better if you can grow as many as possible in your own garden or in pots. This isn't the case because it will necessarily make your magick more powerful or potent. Rather, it's about building a relationship with the Earth and the rest of Nature, communing with the cycles of life, of plants, and of the seasons. If you're able to use herbs you grow yourself, be sure to dry them before use so they're easily crushed with a pestle and mortar.

You can, of course, include other herbs as well. A solar incense doesn't have to be made exclusively of herbs associated with the

Sun. If you love the smell of mint and want to add it, then go for it. But keep in mind too that incense blends created by witches don't always smell pleasant. If you're making a blend for a spell, then you very well may be more interested in the magickal properties of the herbs you're using than how they smell when blended together.

Table 3 below includes a number of incense blends I've created over the years for my own work. Each of them uses herbs associated with the Sun. Feel free to use these recipes exactly as presented, or as inspiration for your own solar incense blends.

Table 3 - Solar Incense Blends

Solar Flare Blend	Combining cinnamon, orange peel, and marigold, this incense blend is a spicy, zesty, and invigorating mix that conjures the radiant energy of the Sun at its zenith. Solarpunk witches can use this blend in rituals to amplify courage, foster positive change, or invoke energetic growth—be it personal, communal, or environmental.
Sunrise Splendor Blend	This blend of chamomile, sunflower seeds, and juniper berries evokes the calm, hopeful energy of a new day's dawn. The soothing scent makes it ideal for morning rituals, setting a positive tone for the day ahead. As a solarpunk witch, you can use this blend to cultivate a fresh perspective, rejuvenate your spirit, or kickstart a new eco-initiative.
Solar Eclipse Blend	Merging oak bark, chrysanthemum petals, and a touch of cinnamon, this blend calls to mind the profound and transformative energy of a solar eclipse. This mix is ideal for rituals that seek to bring about significant transitions or pivotal revelations. As a solarpunk witch, I use this blend when undertaking a big project, like launching a community solar garden or making a significant lifestyle change.

Midsummer Mélange	A combination of sunflower petals, marigold, and orange peel, this incense blend captures the pure joy and abundance of midsummer. Use it in your midsummer rituals to celebrate the Sun at its most potent or anytime you want to invoke feelings of joy, abundance, and warmth. Solarpunk witches can also use this blend when celebrating victories, big or small, in their eco-activism work.
Sundown Serenity Blend	Chamomile, juniper berries, and oak bark come together in this blend to create a calming, grounding aroma reminiscent of the Sun's peaceful descent at the end of the day. Ideal for evening rituals or winding down after a day of activism, this blend helps you tap into the quiet strength and resilience that comes from knowing the Sun will rise again. Solarpunk witches might use this blend for reflection, rest, and recharging their energies for the battles to come.

Solar Oil Blends

Like incense, oil blends use herbs as both their magickal and olfactory base. To make a solar oil blend, you have a few options. One, you can buy essential oils or oil infusions made from the herbs listed above. Generally each oil will be made from one herb, though you can also find oil blends to buy.

Get the oils you need that are made from your choice of solar-associated herbs, then blend those oils together. You don't need a lot of different oils—two or three will do. But you might want to use more, depending on the magickal work you're doing and the other properties you're trying to pull into your blend.

You can also make your own oils, which fits quite well with the DIY solarpunk ethos. To make an oil infusion is quite simple. You'll need the following short list of supplies:

- A mason jar

- Olive oil

- Dried herbs

- Cheesecloth

- Colored glass bottles[70]

To create an infused oil, all you have to do is fill a mason jar with the dried herb of your choice. Then, pour an edible carrier oil like olive oil into the jar until the dried herbs are completely covered. Let it sit in a dark place for an entire lunar cycle. Once that time has passed, use the cheesecloth to strain the infused oil into small, brown glass jars. You can do this with individual herbs, then blend oils together based on the work you're doing. If you plan far enough ahead, you can also create an oil blend all at once by mixing your herbs together in a mason jar before adding oil, instead of only adding one particular herb.

Finally, you can also make essential oils, which is different from an infusion in the process used to extract the oil. It's a more involved and difficult process that involves distillation of steam through tubes. There's a DIY method[71] that uses dried herbs, a crockpot, distilled water, and a refrigerator. You basically slow cook the herbs in distilled water for three or four hours, then put the crockpot in the refrigerator overnight. An oil will form on the top layer that can be scraped off into bottles in addition to small amounts of the liquid from your pot.

Once your blend is finished, then it's ready for use. However you make it, you can use it for cleansing and ritual baths, anointing yourself, and blessing and charging magickal tools—and as an added associative element to charms and other spells, among other uses.

---

70 Note: brown bottles provide the best protection against UV light, which causes oxidation that degrades and breaks down the oils, rendering their physical and spiritual properties less effective. For more information, Carow Packaging's blog has an excellent article on this subject: carowpackaging.com/blog/which-colored-glass-is-best-for-essential-oils.
71 DIYNatural.com has a helpful article about this process: diynatural.com/diy-essential-oils.

Table 4 below is a short sample list of oil infusions using herbs associated with the Sun, with a few quick suggestions for how you can use them in your practice as a solarpunk witch.

Table 4 - Solar Oil Infusions

Bergamot Infusion	With its bright, uplifting citrus scent, bergamot is associated with the warming, invigorating energy of the Sun. The aroma helps to lighten the mood, stimulate positivity, and encourage motivation. As a solarpunk witch, you could use bergamot essential oil in your spellwork and rituals for elevating spirits, inspiring action for eco-activism, or promoting optimism for a sustainable, equitable future. It can also be used to help ease anxiety and stress.
Frankincense Infusion	Known for its rich, earthy, and slightly sweet scent, frankincense is deeply connected to the Sun and has well-documented historic uses in spiritual and meditative practices. The fragrance aids in deepening concentration, enhancing spiritual awareness, and fostering a sense of connectedness. As a solarpunk witch, you could incorporate frankincense essential oil in your meditations for grounding, centering, and connecting with the Sun, or use it in ritual work aimed at galvanizing community resilience and unity.
Lemon Infusion	Lemon oil, with its vibrant and fresh scent, is a potent symbol of the Sun's cleansing and rejuvenating qualities. It's known to stimulate clarity, invigorate the mind, and promote a sense of freshness. As a solarpunk witch, you could use lemon essential oil in your rituals to clear away negativity, inspire new eco-friendly ideas, or encourage clean, sustainable living practices. It can also be added to household cleaners as part of a greener, more Earth-friendly lifestyle.

Stones and Crystals Associated with the Sun

Stones and crystals are another tool witches commonly used for spells and charms, crystal grids, and spiritual healing. Often, people place stones outside overnight in the light of the Moon to charge in the Moon's energy. You can do that with stones associated with the Sun, but you may want to consider charging Sun-associated stones in the Sun's light in addition to or instead of the Moon.

Like herbs and other things used in Craft work, stones have magickal associations with planets, colors, elements, deities, emotions, and more. I tend to use sunstone and clear quartz most often when working with Sun energy, but, through the course of my practice, I've come to associate other stones with the Sun and its energy as well (see the list below). Stones I've come to associate most with the Sun through my own work include amber, citrine, sunstone, golden topaz, heliodor, pyrite, and tiger's eye.

Table 5 - Solar Stones

Amber	Long celebrated for its warm, sun-like hue and its fossil origins, amber carries the ancient energy of the Earth and Sun mingling together. Its powerful connection to life and rebirth makes it a potent tool in any transformative solarpunk work, especially those centered around revitalizing ecosystems or communities.
Citrine	Known as the "success stone" or "merchant's stone," citrine exudes a sunny and optimistic energy that can bolster the confidence and resolve needed for solarpunk projects. It's ideal for any work related to manifesting dreams, promoting abundance, or fostering positive group dynamics.

Sunstone	As its name suggests, sunstone emanates the energy of the radiant sun. It invites feelings of joy and inspires the renewal of life's sweet moments. In solarpunk witchcraft, it can be used in works aimed at spreading happiness, fostering resilience, and igniting passion for causes that matter.
Golden Topaz	This is a crystal of intention, manifestation, and willpower, attributes much needed in the path of a solarpunk witch. It aligns with the sun's energy, fueling the determination to bring about a sustainable future.
Pyrite	Often called "fool's gold," pyrite carries an energy that resonates with the sun. It stimulates creativity, ambition, and determination, making it a powerful aid for solarpunk witches working on long-term projects or in positions of leadership.
Heliodor	Also known as yellow beryl, this stone carries the golden light of the sun. It infuses us with courage, wisdom, and the will to do good—all vital traits for anyone seeking to instigate change and uphold the solarpunk ethos.
Tiger's Eye	A stone of protection and grounding, tiger's eye also harmonizes with solar energies, helping cultivate balance. For solarpunk witches, this could serve as a potent reminder to harmonize technological advancement and Earth-consciousness in their pursuits.

Each of these stones and crystals, in their own unique ways, draws on the power of the sun. Use them to amplify your intentions, fuel your solar rituals, or infuse your daily life with the strength and courage necessary for the monumental task of building a greener, more equitable world. If you're interested in stone magick, you can find a much more comprehensive list of stones and their associations in *Cunningham's Encyclopedia of Crystal, Gem & Metal Magic*.

Solar Archetypes

I don't use deities in my own solarpunk spirituality, but many pagans and witches do use deities either out of tradition, genuine belief, or as symbols and archetypes relevant to their ritual and magick. Even if you're agnostic or atheist, or just prefer not using specific deities, you can still—if you wish—recognize the spirit of mythological deities as universal, perennial archetypes that have much to teach us. A very short and incomplete list of Sun-associated god and goddess archetypes from around the world include the following.[72]

Table 6 - Solar Deity Archetypes

Belinos	A powerful Celtic solar deity, Belinos was venerated throughout ancient Europe for his radiant energy. Known as "the shining one," he represents the glowing vitality and life-giving force of the Sun.
Helios	In ancient Greek mythology, Helios personifies the Sun itself. He's traditionally depicted driving a radiant chariot across the sky each day, illuminating the world and governing the passage of time.
Savitr	An important deity in the Rigveda, one of the ancient Hindu scriptures, Savitr is the god who stimulates all life and brings forth the day with his bright, golden hands.
Ra	Known as the Egyptian Sun god, Ra symbolizes creation, light, and renewal. He was believed to sail across the sky during the day in a solar barque and through the underworld at night, representing the cycle of death and rebirth.

---

72 To aid in your own research, you can find much more comprehensive lists and descriptions at sites such as the following: goddess-guide.com/sun-goddesses.html and historycooperative.org/sun-gods-dieties-of-the-sun/.

Beiwe	This Saami goddess of the sun, spring, fertility, and sanity, is associated with the renewal of the Sun at the Winter Solstice. She brings warmth, light, and sanity back to people and animals after the long, dark winter.
Sol	The personification of the Sun in Roman mythology, Sol drives his chariot across the sky each day just like his Greek counterpart, Helios. He was associated with vision and the unblinking, all-seeing eye of justice.
Nana-huatzin	In Aztec mythology, Nanahuatzin is the humble god who sacrificed himself in fire to become the Sun, symbolizing self-sacrifice, courage, and transformation.
Malina	An Inuit Sun goddess, Malina represents the chase, as she is perpetually pursued by her brother, the Moon. She signifies the endless dance between the Sun and Moon.
Gun Ana	In the mythology of the Chuvash, a Turkic people of Russia, Gun Ana is the Sun mother. She is a source of life, warmth, and fertility, reflecting the nurturing aspect of the Sun.
Lugh	Known as a master of all skills in Irish mythology, Lugh is associated with the Sun, light, and warmth. He embodies the Sun's energy in inspiring craftsmanship, creativity, and prosperity.

Remember, working with deities is a personal journey and there is no right or wrong choice. Choose to work with the deities that resonate with you and align with your solarpunk beliefs and practices. Personally, I'm very conscious of cultural appropriation, and most other solarpunks tend to be as well, at least I hope. For this reason, I generally work only with deities from cultures I have roots in, primarily Celtic and Nordic.

If you do choose to work with deities outside your cultural ancestry, please approach those cultural deities with respect, acknowledging the historical and cultural contexts in which they were originally worshiped, and acknowledging the hierarchical and imperialist power relationships that exist throughout the world as a result of centuries of western imperialism.

SUN MAGICK

Creating a Sun Altar

Altars are a great way to bring magick into our everyday lives. The altars we create in our homes help emphasize our dwellings as sacred space. With solarpunk's emphasis on solutions to the global problems we face on the planet Earth, solarpunk witches might have a general Craft altar or even an altar dedicated specifically to the Earth.

Solarpunk witches may also want to have an altar dedicated to the Sun. It doesn't have to be large or take up a lot of space, though it certainly can if you want. It also doesn't need to have a large number of items or cost a lot of money.

To create a Sun altar, find a flat space somewhere in your house that you don't need for other uses. Put an altar cloth down on the surface, then arrange the items you've collected for your Sun altar. There are standard altar placements for a lot of items and tools, like the pentacle, element symbols, deity/archetype candles, etc. Butstandard placements aren't rules. Feel free to arrange your altar in whatever way feels best to you.

The following are items associated with the Sun that you may want to place on your altar. None of these are necessary or required. Choose items that appeal to you, that resonate with you and have meaning for you. Choose items that help you connect with the Sun and Sun energy.

Table 7 - Sun Altar Items

Altar Cloth	Any kind of cloth will do long as it's large enough for the altar you want to build. Orange, red, or yellow cloth, or any combination of those colors, works well for a Sun altar.
Candles	Choose candles with colors like orange, red, and yellow that are associated with solar energy. You could even find a Sun-shaped candle.
Sun Symbols	This could include images of the Sun and fire (which is also physically present when you light your candles), any small items shaped like the Sun, and images or small statues representing Sun deities/archetypes.
Incense	Use an incense made from a blend of herbs associated with the Sun (see page 120). You can also use a small flame-activated oil diffuser with an essential oil solar blend.
Flowers	Feel free to decorate your altar with flowers as well. Sunflowers or other flowers that resemble the Sun such as gazania, black-eyed susan, calendula, and African marigold are among a wide variety of flowers that resemble the Sun in both shape and color.
Stones and Crystals	Heliolite, also known as sunstone, is a great semi-precious gem you can use to decorate your Sun altar. You could also use quartz, peridot, citrine, amber, or any other stones associated with the Sun's energy.

The above list is by no means exhaustive, and you should feel free to always be adding to the list of possibilities as you come across things that remind you of Sun energy. Other examples could include images or representations of the Phoenix, the Sun and/or Chariot tarot cards, Sun-colored ribbons, food, and more. The only limit is your own imagination and sense of what fits within your conception of the idea of Sun energy.

Communing with the Sun

Invocations or evocations are a common part of pagan and witchcraft rituals that can be done regardless of whether or not you believe in deities. If you are a theist, you can invoke appropriate deities for your work. If you're an agnostic or atheist, then you can invoke or evoke symbolism, energies, and archetypes. Whatever you believe or don't, the following invocation invites the Sun and its energy into your ritual and magickal space.

Drawing down the Moon is a common ritual tradition among many Wiccan groups, and is essentially a Moon invocation in which a priestess invites the power and energy of the Moon Goddess into her and to speak through her. You can find various versions of the ritual, including one that appears in Gerald Gardner's 1949 book, *The Gardnerian Book of Shadows*.[73] But as stated above, all versions amount to invoking the power of the Moon to use during a ritual and in working magick.

The communing with the Sun ritual is inspired by the drawing down the Moon ritual with important differences. One, of course, is that we're working with the Sun rather than the Moon. Another difference is that communing with the Sun isn't about having a deity speak through you. Rather, it's about welcoming, experiencing, and communing with Sun energy and learning to integrate it into your life.

You may want to do either rituals centered on communing with the Sun or the Moon—or even both, for the sake of balance in your spiritual practice. But communing with the Sun is something all solarpunk witches should know how to do, and can be used during the invocation portion of the general solarpunk ritual or as a stand alone, daily ritual practice. Whatever frequency with which you choose to practice this ritual, it's meant as a means of connecting

---

73 You can access this text here: sacred-texts.com/pag/gbos/gbos01.htm.

to and building a more harmonious relationship with the Sun and its energy.

Sun altar (illustration by Aspen Muskovich)

The Ritual

Face the midday Sun and perform your inner grove or sacred space meditation to ground and center yourself and get yourself into a ritual state of mind. Once you're ready, cleanse the space, cast a circle, and call the quarters according to the basic ritual for solarpunk witches format outlined in Chapter Four, or using a ritual outline of our own creation.

When you get to the invocation section of the basic ritual for solarpunk witches, facing the Sun, stand with your feet shoulder width apart. You can also sit if you need to, or even if you just want to. Raise your hands above your head and repeat the following Sun Energy Invocation (or one of your own creation):

As the Sun, in its unwavering journey, ascends the celestial dome, painting the world in brilliant hues of life and light, so may its resplendent rays illuminate my being. Bathed in the golden aurora of dawn, I stand before you, a humble vessel seeking your radiance.

You, who charts the course of the day, driving back the night and birthing dawn, let your vitality seep into my essence. As a field absorbs your touch, sprouting forth in verdant glory, may I too drink from your eternal wellspring of energy, growing in strength and purpose.

Mighty Sun, in all your golden majesty, spark that kindles life, beacon that guides us from the abyss, I welcome your luminary wisdom. Descend upon me, permeate me with your radiant energy. Just as you rise each day, unwavering in your resolve, inspire me to rise to my own challenges, persistent in my efforts, resilient in my spirit.

Glorious Sun, by the power of your scorching ardor and steady journey across the sky, I seek to mirror your unwavering strength and courage. As the world basks in your golden glow, imbibe in me your luminous lessons. Let me stand firm in my own light, shine in my own strength, and be guided by your eternal wisdom.

Your journey is a dance of resilience and renewal, a testament to the constancy of change. As you give life to the Earth, let your light fill me, empower me, and guide me. As you are the life-giver, the illuminator of paths, I welcome you, I invoke you, I am one with you, under your glowing mantle of power, warmth, and possibility.

Feel and visualize the warm, electric, powerful light of the Sun pouring into your body through your hands and head. It fills your being completely and fully, and all your senses awaken with a jolt like a bolt of lightning striking your heart.

You can also capture the light of the Sun in a chalice or jar of water during this ritual. Then, you can drink it, use it for bathing, use it to cleanse and charge magickal tools, or store it for future use. If you feel any feelings or if words of wisdom and inspiration come to you, then speak them and write them down, or otherwise record them for later reflection and meditation.

Sun Bathing

A great method of cleansing yourself and getting into the right frame of mind for workingSun magick is to Sunbathe as part of your ritual preparation. Take time to bask in the Sun's sparkling and abundant light as it pours down around you and through you. Speak and write down any words of inspiration that spring to mind, ask for any guidance or wisdom, or simply enjoy the connection. You may wish to use this time to perform specific solar magic, casting spells or setting intentions that align with the Sun's qualities of strength, courage, vitality, and success.

Charging Ritual Tools with Sun Energy

While you're performing the communing with the Sun ritual, it's a perfect time to charge your magickal tools with the Sun's energy. It's common for witches to charge tools with the Moon's light and energy, and if you're a solarpunk witch, you can also do the same thing with the Sun. Of course, being a solarpunk witch doesn't mean you can't use the Moon or other planets in your magick as well.

You can charge many useful things with the energy of the Sun: altar tools like your athame, wand, pentagram, chalice, ritual candles, incense blends, water, salt, and other items.[74]

To charge an object with the Sun's energy, you can simply leave it outside directly in the Sun to soak up the rays. You can keep it out all day, or if you want to capture the essence of a particular phase of the Sun, you can leave it out for the morning, midday,[75]

---

74 Don't set essential oils or oil infusions out in sunlight for any length of time. UV light breaks down oils and weakens their scents and effectiveness.

75 In this context, midday does not refer to 12:00 p.m. Rather, it refers to the halfway point between sunrise and sunset. If the Sun rises at 6:00 a.m. and sets at 6:00 p.m., then noon is, in fact, midday. However, if the Sun rises at 8:00 a.m. and sets at 4:00 p.m., then midday would be at 1:00 p.m. Here in the Pacific Northwest during the summer, the Sun rises around 5:30 a.m. and sets around 9:00 p.m. That's sixteen hours of daylight around the Summer Solstice. In that case, midday is, roughly, around 1:30

or afternoon/early evening and bring it back in at the onset of the next phase. If you don't want to leave it out all day, but still want the strongest possible charge, then set it out midday when the Sun's strength is at its peak. You could also choose a Sunday, which is quite literally the Sun's day, the day of the week astrologically ruled by the Sun. See Table 1 on page 118 for information on the daily Sun phases and their magickal correspondence.

Solar Divination

Divination is a common practice among pagans, witches, and many others who practice a variety of spiritual paths. You may already have ideas churning in your mind about how you can use the Sun and its energy in your divination practice, and, of course, there are numerous ways in which solarpunk witches can do so. We'll briefly review a few of those here.

Pendulum

If you practice pendulum divination, you can dress and bless your pendulum with Sun water (see page 138) and a solar incense blend. Another option is to make a pendulum using a crystal or stone associated with the Sun. For example, clear crystal pendulums are easily found to purchase, and the crystals themselves are readily found and affordable if you want to make your own.

Scrying

Below, we'll discuss how to go about solarpunk scrying for divination.

But an important note before we go on: Never look directly into the Sun. It will blind you, likely permanently. So just don't. In fact, don't even look near the Sun either. Looking at the Sun in any way, shape, or form is not required for solar scrying.

Instead, there are a number of different ways to use the Sun for scrying.

---

p.m. Regardless of the exact time, however, in most locales around the world, midday will come sometime around the noon hour, even if not exactly on the dot.

1. You can use a flame as a symbolic substitute for the Sun. After all, the Sun is quite literally made of fire more intense than we can comprehend. To use this method, simply stare into a bonfire, cauldron fire, or candle flame and divine what can be seen, experienced, and learned from inside the inferno.

2. You can also use one of the most widely known methods of scrying, the crystal ball. To use your crystal ball for solar scrying, take your orb outside into the Sun rather than sitting inside. Find a place where the Sun's rays can be absorbed and reflected by your crystal ball, but where the light won't be reflected back into your eyes. You may have to adjust the ball as the Sun moves, depending on your particular location, but I do this often and have found it to be not only safe, but also quite captivating, beautiful, and magickal. However, if you're worried about what this might do to your eyes, you can still use your crystal ball outside while sitting in the shade, or you can—as mentioned above—substitute a candle for the Sun. Either way, stare into the ball of crystal and see what the Sun has to tell and teach you.

3. Sit outside facing the Sun, but, as always, don't look directly into the Sun. Look straight ahead into the direction of the Sun and squint—close your eyes as much as possible without completely cutting off your vision. The Sunlight will play games and tricks with you through its interaction with your eyelashes, your partially covered eyes, and the objects in your narrowed field of vision. Observe this interplay. What messages and insights do you glean?

To reiterate, there are two key safety practices to remember when doing this exercise:

> **A. Do not ever look directly into the Sun.** Doing so can easily harm your eyes and blind you.

B. Be sure to squint. Your eyes should only barely be open. This both helps protect your eyes and skews the Sun's rays in a way that enables scrying.

SUN SPELLS AND MAGICKAL METHODOLOGIES

The following is a series of more concrete examples of how the Sun and Sun energy can be woven into your specific spellwork, regardless of whether or not that work is political and activist in nature. You'll find ways to work Sun energy into your sigils, charm bags, and candle, crystal, and culinary magick. You'll also learn how to do releasing and rebirth and new beginning spells.

Sun Water

Sun water is a valuable and easy-to-make resource for your magickal practice. You can use Sun water to bless and cleanse yourself, your tools, and your fellow solarpunk witches. It can also be used to dress your candles,[76] as a base ingredient for potions, to clear and cleanse sacred space, in banishing rituals, or in just about any other type of magickal spell and practice that uses water. You can always utilize Sun water for additional power and magickal correspondence in your solarpunk craft or other magickal work.

Supplies:

- A mason jar with lid
- Clean water

Fill the mason jar with clean water. If you aren't sure whether the water is clean or not, you can filter it to eliminate particulates and boil it to eliminate any bacteria that could potentially harm you before using it in your magickal work.

With your jar filled about eighty percent of the way to the top, set it on your altar. Pick up your athame and hold it above your

---

76 Dressing a candle simply means to spread a magickal substance, such as essential oils or infused water, over the candles.

head. Take a deep breath and slowly bring the athame, point down,
into the jar of water and say something like,

> *By the powers of Earth, Air, Fire, and Water,*
>
> *By the Spirits of renewal and rejuvenation,*
>
> *I bless this water for use in my magickal work.*
>
> *Blessed Be.*

Take your jar outside and leave it in the Sun for the whole day.
Then, bring it inside and keep it somewhere relatively dark and
cool. Use as needed.

Solar Candle Magick

The following candle magick spell is meant to be general purpose.
Feel free to use it as is, modify it, or use it as inspiration to write your
own unique spell. This spell can be used to manifest any intention,
especially if it's related in some way to Sun energy.

Supplies:

- A solar-colored candle or candles (orange, red, yellow)
- Your choice of herbs that are associated with the intention
  of your spell. These herbs can also have a shared solar
  association, but most important for this spell is that they
  represent your intention.
- Pestle and mortar
- Non-toxic glitter glue
- A lighter or matches

In this spell, you mix your intention-imbued herbs with the solar
candle and then burn it all the way down. While doing so, visualize
your intention. Visualize the power of the Sun helping to manifest
your intention. If you want, you can dress and bless your candle
ahead of time with solar water and solar-associated essential oils.

There are a variety of ways you can combine your herbs and
candle. The easiest way is to grind up your herbs with pestle and

mortar and simply sprinkle the herbs around your candle. In this case, you won't necessarily be burning the herbs, but their energy is combined with that of the solar candle through proximity.

A second way is to prep your candle ahead of time by using a non-toxic golden glitter glue to basically baste the herbs onto the outside of your candle. Set the candle out in the Sun to dry and soak up more Sun energy. When you burn the candle and do your visualization, the herbs representing your intention will then burn along with the solar candle.

A third way, and the last we'll go through here, is to use a Sun-colored pillar candle made from soy wax.[77] Use your boline to dig wax out of the center-top of the candle, forming a small bowl or crater around the top of the wick. Fill this space with your herbs. Next, melt the wax you dug out of the top of the candle, and then pour as much of the melted wax as you can back into the top of the candle and over the herbs. Take care not to cover the top inch of the wick or spill wax on it. Once the wax dries, the candle is ready to use to activate your spell whenever you want. When you light it, the fire from the wick will melt the wax, burn the herbs, and release their odor along with your spell.

Solar Powered Sigils

Sigils, a fancy magickal term for a symbolic and often pictorial representation of the desired outcome for a magickal work, have a long history. In Iceland, for example, staves were and are a common form of sigil magick, for example.[78] Even in the modern world, sigils have become popularized and more common by their use in chaos magick.

Supplies:

- Parchment paper

---

77 Pillar candles work much better for this craft than taper candles because pillar candles have wide and relatively flat surfaces, whereas taper candles end in a point.
78 For those who want to learn more about Icelandic staves, a great starting point is icelandrovers.is/blog/the-magical-staves-of-iceland.

- Pencil or pen

The easiest way to work Sun energy into your sigil magick is to draw a Sun like the ones in Figure 1 or 2 below, and use it to frame your sigil. In addition, you can draw other symbols associated with the Sun into your sigil. Examples of such symbols might include, but certainly aren't limited to a wheel, an ankh, or circular discs. Sun energy can be infused into any sigil you're making for an intention that's related to the meaning and symbolism of the Sun.

Once you've created a sigil, you want to release and launch its power into the universe so it can manifest in the physical realm. There are a variety of ways this can be accomplished. The most common, and the one that probably aligns most with solarpunk witchcraft, is to burn the paper on which the sigil is drawn.

Another way to release a sigil's power is to use a hammer or similar tool to destroy the sigil. This works best if you've created a sigil that is more three dimensional than drawing on paper. For example, you might use a block of wood to carve something as a physical manifestation of your intention, focusing on that intention and imbuing the wood with that intention as you carve. Then to release the sigil's power, you would smash the carving with a hammer. Of course, with a woodcarving, you could also burn it the same way you would a sigil drawing. You could also turn food into sigils and release the intention through eating (see the solar culinary magick section on page 145).

Solar Stone Magick

Stones and crystals are often used in spiritual healing. Witches also carry stones or crystals with them that are associated with certain properties they wish to bring into their lives. You can also use stones in charms and other kinds of magick.

One of the magickal properties of the Sun is creativity. This comes through the Sun's obvious association with fire, which represents drive, passion, and the spark of creative inspiration. The following then is a solar spell to bring creativity that utilizes stone magick.

Supplies:

- A clear glass jar and lid
- Water
- A stone or crystal associated with the Sun. If you can find a solar stone that is also specifically associated with encouraging or enhancing creativity in any way, even better. For example, pyrite is a stone that's associated with the Sun and therefore creativity, and also encourages manifestation and abundance.

Fill your glass jar with water. Then take the jar and your pyrite outside in the morning Sun. Sunrise or close to it is the ideal Sun phase for new ideas, inspiration, and sparking creativity.

Take your stone and—with your hands cupped like a chalice— hold it up above your head in the magickal light of the Sun and say,

Great and mighty Sun
Imbue this stone with inspiration
And the spark of creative fire.
So mote it be!

Place the stone in the jar of water and starting at sunrise, let it sit for about three hours in the early morning Sun, until the transition from the sunrise to the morning Sun phase. Then take the jar in your hands and say,

I drink this solar water
Infusing myself with inspiration
And the spark of creative fire.
So mote it be!

Figure 1: Sun-framed sigil example (illustration by Justine Norton-Kertson)

Figure 2: Another sun-framed sigil example (illustration by Justine Norton-Kertson)

Take a drink of the water. You don't have to drink all of it, but you can if you'd like. Then take the stone out of the jar, and, if there's any water left, pour it out onto the Earth. Keep the stone with you to inspire creativity, especially when you're engaging in creative or artistic activities.

Solar Charm Bag

Charm bags can be made for any variety of intentions. If there are any magickal properties associated with the Sun that you want to bring into or expand in your life, you can make a charm bag composed of Sun-associated ingredients. For this example, we'll make a charm bag to increase self-confidence.

As with the solar stone spell above, you can use any ingredients associated with the Sun, as they'll carry the magickal property of self-confidence with them to at least some degree. Potential items to add to your charm bag include any of the following:

- Herbs that correspond with Sun energy

- Stones that correspond with Sun energy

- Essential oils that correspond with Sun energy

- Small images, statues, or other symbolic representations of the Sun

You can refer back to Chapter Five for magickal solar correspondences. Enhance the Sun energy of your spell by finding ingredients that both correspond with the Sun *and also* are specifically associated with self-confidence or related characteristics like courage.

If you have trouble finding herbs, stones, or other ingredients to buy that are associated with both the Sun and self-confidence simultaneously, then you can use some ingredients that correspond to the Sun on the one hand, and others that correspond to self-confidence on the other, even if they have no direct Sun correspondence. For example, garlic is associated with inner strength, but not with the Sun.

Once you've found your ingredients, mix them together in your charm bag. You can also further enhance your charm by including an ingredient or two that enhances the power of spells. Another example is carnation petals, which both enhance the power of magick and are one of the flowers associated with the Sun. You can use fresh or dried petals.

An example of a solar charm bag to increase self-confidence is a bag that includes carnation petals to enhance the spell's magick, as well as goldstone, heliodor, and golden topaz stones, all of which are associated with both the Sun and confidence. Also included are tarragon, an herb that increases self-confidence, and nasturtium, which is an herb that aids with releasing fear. Also included are a small gold-plated Sun-shaped bracelet charm and a small chunk of wax charged in the midday Sun. Finally, our example charm bag also has a small ankh inside it, which is a symbol of the Egyptian Sun god Ra.

Carry the charm bag around with you to help increase your self-confidence.

Solar Culinary Magick

Culinary magick is a subset of witchcraft revolving around the spiritual and magickal properties of food. It involves imbuing meals with intention during preparation and consumption, and thereby transforming the act of eating into a sacred ritual and act of magickal power. Rooted in the kitchen witch tradition, culinary magick also aligns wonderfully with solarpunk's DIY spirit.[79] In solarpunk witchcraft, culinary magick is not only a means of

---

79 Kitchen witches don't often bother with the excesses of ritual, nor do they tend to have fancy magical tools bought at high end pagan shops. (I'm not throwing shade on anyone here. I have fancy tools myself. For example, my boline is a crescent shaped stainless steel blade with a polished wood and mother of pearl hilt, which is hardly a standard kitchen knife.) Rather, kitchen witches, in true, solarpunk DIY fashion, use whatever happens to be on hand (whether or not it's found in a kitchen) when needed to perform their magickal spells. For the kitchen witch, then, a butter or steak knife is a tool used to prepare and eat food, as well as an athame, if they should ever need or want to use one.

personal empowerment and spiritual connection to the earth, but also a vehicle for community-building and activism.

For the solarpunk witch, the kitchen itself becomes an altar upon which we do our work. The process of preparing food is transformed into a magickal spell in itself. The selection of ingredients, chopping, stirring, simmering—each act, each stage of the cooking process, becomes a part of the ritual, imbued with intention and power. Food grown sustainably, whether from one's garden or sourced from local, ethical farmers, becomes a physical representation of solarpunk values. Each ingredient carries the energy of the Sun, Earth, Water, and Air, tying us back to the Earth, the four elements, and the cycle of life.

When preparing food with a specific intention in mind, solarpunk witches incorporate ingredients corresponding to that intention. For example, basil and cinnamon might be used for a spell for prosperity since those two herbs correspond with both the Sun and the concept of prosperity. Similarly, rosemary and thyme might be added to a dish meant for protection. The act of eating then becomes a way of drawing these energies into ourselves, physically integrating the magick we perform into our own bodies.

One way I like to approach culinary magick is as an edible form of sigil magick. When looked at from this perspective, the food I prepare and fill with my intention becomes a physical manifestation of the symbol (rather than a drawing). The act of eating that food becomes my method of launching the sigil's power and intention into the universe.

For solarpunk witches though, magick isn't just about personal empowerment; it's about creating a better world, which means building and nurturing resilient communities. Here, the true potential of solarpunk culinary magick shines. Sharing meals is a universal act of community and connection. Baking bread with the intention of building unity and then sharing that bread at a community gathering, for example, can be a powerful act of magick that helps reinforce the bonds of community, spreading the intention of unity to all who partake of the bread.

Similarly, bringing intention-filled foods to protests, rallies, and organizing meetings can serve multiple purposes. It provides physical nourishment, which is often much needed in situations of intense grassroots organizing and activity. But beyond that, it also serves to ground the group's intention, to provide a moment of unity and connection and fellowship, to physically embody the changes they're working towards. Imagine a pot of soup prepared with the intention of fostering justice, or cookies baked with the intention of spreading compassion and peace, shared among the attendees. This isn't just symbolic—it's magick that everyone can taste.

Culinary magick is an accessible and potent form of witchcraft, perfectly suited to the solarpunk ethos. By combining sustainability, community-building, and magick, it offers a practical way to manifest solarpunk values in daily life.

Solar Release Spell

The following spell uses Sun energy as a base of power to release things in your life that are holding you back or that for one reason or another no longer serve you and your best interest. The spell can be timed with days and times relevant to the Sun in order to enhance the magick. For example, you could perform the spell on a Sunday, which is the day of the Sun. You could also perform the spell at sunset, which is an ideal time of the day for solar release magick.[80]

Supplies:

- Solar colored candle

- Slips of parchment paper

- A pen or pencil

---

80 See Table 1 on page 118 for a correspondence table on the daily Sun phases and working magic.

- Your cauldron

- A solar oil blend that also contains the properties of releasing and letting go

- A lighter or matches

Dress your solar colored candle with the solar oil blend, then light the candle. Use the pen and parchment to write down things you want to release. Then, much like a sigil spell, take each slip of parchment and burn them one at a time with the candle's flame. Once you've lit a piece of parchment on fire, place it in the cauldron and focus on your intention as it burns. Repeat with the other slips of paper.

Rebirth and New Beginnings Spell

Like any other spellwork, there are a wide variety of magickal methodologies you can use for a rebirth or new beginnings spell. You could:

- visualize your successful and fruitful new beginning and draw it into a sigil,

- make a charm bag to carry around, or

- perform the releasing spell above but tailor it for new beginnings.

  - Simply write down on a slip of parchment your vision for a new beginning, or write down whatever it is you want to bring into your life as you make a fresh start. Then burn that slip of parchment in the fire as you visualize your successful new beginning.

Another great way to perform a Sun-focused new beginnings or fresh start spell is to incorporate the phoenix—a powerful symbol of rebirth. For example, you could perform a spell where you light some solar colored candles, burn a solar incense blend, and quietly meditate on the phoenix, its meaning, and its purpose in your life at that particular moment.

Speak to the phoenix, share with it your dreams, desires, and aspirations for your rebirth and new beginning. Then watch it carry your dreams through the flames, burn away, and be reborn anew in the image of your vision for a fresh start. Watch the newly born phoenix as it rises from the ashes and flames.

Feel yourself rising from the ashes and flames, reborn and ready to start again, for you are the phoenix.

●   ●   ●

The practices and rituals solarpunk witches employ harness the energy of the Sun for spiritual and magickal purposes. In this last chapter, we worked through various Sun meditations, examined the significance of Sun correspondences in spellwork, the use of herbs, stones, and incense blends associated with the Sun, and the creation of solar altars. We emphasized the Sun's role in solarpunk witchcraft as a symbol of vitality, creativity, and transformation, providing detailed guidance on integrating solar energy into daily practices and rituals. By doing so, we can foster a deeper connection with nature and personal empowerment in our lives and our Craft practice.

Chapter Seven: Earth Magick for Solarpunk Witches

*A*s solarpunk witches, we honor the Sun for its life-giving radiance and for the abundance of power and energy it provides us. But we also pay homage to the very ground beneath our feet, the nurturer of life, the great, living entity that sustains us—our Earth. Here, as we did with the Sun in the previous chapter, we'll explore Earth-based meditations, spells, and correspondences that align with our vision for a sustainable and equitable future.

Vast landscapes, a multitude of ecosystems, incredible biodiversity—the Earth is a rich tapestry of living beings and energies and spirits. Its diverse elements, from soil to stones and from plants to animals, carry with them a unique vibration, an essence that can be harnessed and directed towards the realization of our solarpunk aspirations.

The meditations in this chapter will guide you in grounding your energies, connecting deeply with the Earth, and drawing strength and wisdom from its core. You will learn to find stillness in the whisper of the leaves, resilience in the steadfastness of the mountains, and creativity in the playfulness of the babbling brooks.

Our exploration of Earth-based spells will weave together the natural elements at our disposal, drawing on the inherent magick found in herbs, stones, and the soil itself. From prosperity spells that seek to dismantle oppressive economic systems to healing rituals that draw on the nurturing energy of the Earth, these workings will not only empower you as an individual but also serve the broader vision of solarpunk.

In this chapter, you'll also find a variety of correspondences throughout to provide you with a start to your own list of Earth-associated symbols, tools, and elements. Whether it's stones that vibrate with grounding energy or plants that carry the essence of transformation, understanding these correspondences will prove invaluable as you integrate Earth magick into your solarpunk practice.

This chapter is an invitation to touch the Earth, to understand its language, and to draw upon its energy. It's a call to remember our inherent connection to the land, and to work in partnership with it, not only in our magickal practice but in our fight for a greener, more equitable world. So, let's take this journey together, and discover the profound wisdom and potent magick the Earth offers us.

EARTH MEDITATIONS

The Earth is an amazing, powerful, and grounding force. Getting in touch and communing with the Earth through meditation, visualization, and direct experience are vital to the solarpunk witch. Among other purposes, we use Earth meditations to relax and ground us, to fill our beings with power and energy with which to work out magick, and to foster a harmonious relationship with our ecosystem and natural environment.

The Inner Grove meditation outlined in Chapter Four on page 65 is a great example of a meditation and visualization that utilizes Earth energy. Below are a few other examples of Earth-focused meditations I use regularly to bring us into closer connection and relationship with the Earth.

Earth Meditation #1: The Seed—Grounding and Centering

Begin by finding a quiet, comfortable space where you won't be disturbed. You may choose to sit on a cushion, a chair, or directly on the ground. Close your eyes and take several deep, slow breaths to settle your body and quiet your mind.

Visualize yourself as a seed, nestled in the rich, nurturing soil of Mother Earth. Feel the cool, comforting darkness envelop you. Breathe in the scent of damp earth and decaying leaves, the scent of life in its most primal form.

Now, in your mind's eye, see a green sprout emerging from the seed, your seed. As you exhale, envision this sprout growing downwards, forming a strong, sturdy root. With each breath, feel this root burrowing deeper and deeper into the soil.

As you continue to breathe deeply, visualize this root drawing energy up from the heart of the Earth. This energy is solid, bright, grounding, and empowering. Feel it climbing up your root, towards your seed-self, saturating you with the Earth's strength and stability.

Now, imagine the energy sparking a change in your seed-self. A green shoot begins to emerge, reaching upwards, seeking the Sun. As you inhale, the shoot grows taller, stronger. As you exhale, your roots delve deeper, anchoring you firmly to the Earth.

Feel the balance between the upward growth and the downward anchoring. This is the dance of life, the rhythm of existence. Feel the energy of the Earth flowing through you, grounding you, centering you.

Now, picture a leaf unfurling from your shoot, reaching out towards the world, ready to contribute to the solarpunk vision you carry. Hold this image in your mind, feeling the power and potential within you.

Begin to draw your awareness back to your physical body, carrying the grounding energy of the Earth with you. Wiggle your fingers, wiggle your toes, and, when you feel ready, gently open your eyes.

Carry this feeling of groundedness and connection with you throughout your day. Remember, you are as much a part of the Earth as the Earth is a part of you. Use this connection to fuel your actions, to drive your intentions, and to nourish your solarpunk dreams.

Earth Meditation #2: Communing with the Element of Earth

In this meditation, we'll be focusing on our relationship with the element of Earth, not just as a provider of resources, but as a living, breathing entity with whom we share an intimate and harmonious bond. The Earth is more than just dirt beneath our feet; it is the foundation of life, the keeper of ancient wisdom, and the testament of time. This meditation invites us to embody the spirit of a tree in a solarpunk city, a being that is at once a product of the Earth's nurturing and a steward of sustainable technology. Through this journey, we'll connect with the timelessness of the Earth, our place within it, and our responsibility to maintain its balance in our quest for a greener future.

Find a quiet, comforting space where you won't be disturbed, preferably outdoors, where you can touch the Earth directly. Sit or lay down on the ground, allowing your body to make contact with the soil, the grass, or the sand. If you need to use a pillow to sit on, that's perfectly okay.

Close your eyes and begin to attune your breathing to the slow, deep rhythm of the Earth's heartbeat. Visualize yourself as a magnificent, ancient old growth tree rooted in the center of a vibrant, solarpunk cityscape. Your roots reach deep into the soil, twining around crystals and ancient stone, sipping from the depths of subterranean aquifers. Above, your branches stretch high, your leaves shimmering with photosynthetic solar panels that glitter and gleam in the sunlight.

Feel your roots draw energy and nutrients from the soil. Every microorganism, every mineral—they all contribute to your life force, demonstrating the Earth's bounty and interconnectedness. This energy travels up through your roots, spreading into your trunk and branching out into your limbs. You're a bridge between the terrestrial and the celestial, your body a testament to Earth's creative power.

Imagine each of your leaves as small power plants, converting sunlight into energy, feeding both your growth and the community around you. Your existence is a testament to coexistence and mutual aid, a beacon of the balance between nature and technology. You are not merely surviving; you are thriving, and so is the environment around you.

Now, allow your consciousness to descend into your roots. Feel the coolness of the soil, the vibrant life teeming beneath the surface. You're now part of the complex web of life that is the Earth, connected to everything that is, was, and will be. Feel the wisdom and timelessness of the Earth, the stories she carries in her depths. Stay in this place for as long as you'd like, communing with the deep beauty and power of the Earth.

Finally, let your awareness rise once more out from the depths of the rock and soil. Up into your glittering leaves, feel the warm Sun on your bark. Contemplate your place within this world, as a steward of the Earth, a mediator between the natural world and the realm of human ingenuity. Know that every choice, every action, ripples outwards, impacting the world.

Hold this connection with Earth, this sense of purpose and unity. Revel in it for as long as you'd like. And when you're ready, gently start to bring your awareness back to your physical body. As you open your eyes, remember your tree-self and the lessons it holds. Carry these insights into your daily life as a solarpunk witch, fostering a future where sustainability and technology walk hand in hand.

Earth Meditation #3: The Earth Is Water

The Earth is approximately seventy-one percent water. Given that fact, it's hard to focus on the Earth without spending time building a relationship with water. With so many justice issues related to water—such as Indigenous rights and sovereignty and fossil fuel infrastructure like pipelines or oil spills in the ocean—this relationship with water is particularly meaningful for solarpunk witches.

In the following meditation, we explore the vital, life-sustaining power of water within the realm of Earth. As an essential element of our world that connects every landmass on the planet, water serves as a reminder of our interconnectedness, adaptability, and the cyclical nature of life. Let's tap into the flowing, healing, and nurturing properties of water in this unique, Earth-based meditation, designed to inspire and awaken the solarpunk spirit.

Begin in a comfortable position, closing your eyes and taking a few moments to ground yourself. If you're able to be outside near a body of water, that's great, but not necessary. Being comfortable and in the right frame of mind is more important.

Feel the solid Earth beneath you, steady and supportive, soft but firm, warm but cool. You're standing on the shore of a vast ocean. Smell the salty sea breezethat mingles with the warmth of the Sun on your skin. Hear the rhythmic pulse of the waves as they crash and recede—a rhythmic dance, a timeless ebb and flow.

Visualize a river originating from the ocean, its azure waters winding and twisting through diverse landscapes of forests, mountains, and plains. This river is a lifeline, linking all life forms, communities, and habitats together in a grand, interconnected web of existence. This river is the water cycle, a perpetual symbol of renewal and rebirth.

As you follow the river, observe how it nurtures the lands it traverses, giving life and vitality wherever it flows. Its currents shape landscapes, carving valleys and filling basins, symbolizing its dynamic power to reshape and adapt. Its cascading waterfalls and gentle ripples reflect the diversity of our experiences, the highs and lows, the stillness and turmoil.

Now, envision yourself stepping into the river, feeling the cool, invigorating water envelope your feet. With each heartbeat, let the water's purifying energy cleanse your worries, doubts, and fears. As the water flows around you, absorb its resilience and adaptability, let it guide you in navigating the currents of change in your own life.

As the Sun shines overhead, the river sparkles, illuminating a rainbow of colors on its surface, a reminder of the dazzling possibilities that arise when we harness solar energy in harmony with nature's elements. Stay in this place of cleansing for as long as you need. Let the water refresh and renew you, your life, and your spirit.

When you're ready, gradually, pull your attention back to your body and your surroundings, bringing with you the energy and lessons of the water. As you open your eyes, carry the river's wisdom within you—its interconnectedness, its adaptability, its life-sustaining force. You are part of this magnificent cycle, a solarpunk witch drawing power from the harmony of Earth's elements.

Remember that this water, which connects all life, is a resource that needs our protection and respect. Let this meditation inspire you to take actionable steps towards water conservation, clean energy, and fostering a sustainable world. Let the water's wisdom guide your solarpunk witchcraft, as you work towards healing the Earth and its waters.

Blessed Be.

EARTH CORRESPONDENCES FOR SOLARPUNK MAGICK

It's entirely possible to make a convincing argument that all herbs, stones, and similar things are associated with the Earth. After all, here we are, here they are, literally on and of the Earth. Still, as with the other elements, specific herbs, stones, etc. are more closely associated with Earth energy than with say, the elements Fire or Air. Below, I talk about some of things that I've come to associate most with Earth energy through use in my own solarpunk witchcraft practice.

Herbs and Incense Associated with the Earth

The Earth element in witchcraft is associated with grounding, prosperity, abundance, healing, and fertility. In the realm of solarpunk witchcraft, this translates to the nurturing of equitable and sustainable systems, and the grounding of our aspirations for a better world into tangible actions. Certain herbs, due to their properties and associations, are particularly linked with the Earth element. These herbs can be used in a variety of ways in your solarpunk magickal practice. Table 8 below outlines a few examples:

Table 8 — Herbs for Earthy Incense[81]

Patchouli	Known for its deep, earthy scent, patchouli is a powerful grounding herb. It's often used in prosperity spells and rituals, which makes it a valuable ally in solarpunk workings that aim to envision and manifest a post-scarcity economy.
Comfey	This plant is associated with healing, which ties in well with solarpunk's focus on repairing the damage done to our planet and communities. It can be used in spells or rituals intended to promote ecological restoration and social healing.
Sage	Although sage is widely known for its cleansing properties, it also has strong Earth associations. It can be used to purify and ground your space before solarpunk ritual work, creating a clean slate for transformative intentions.
Alfalfa	Traditionally used for protection and prosperity, alfalfa can be used in solarpunk spellwork to help protect vulnerable ecosystems and promote abundance that doesn't harm the planet.
Oak	Oak is a symbol of strength, stability, and wisdom. Use oak in your solarpunk practices when you need to manifest resilience and grounded wisdom in your environmental activism.

These herbs can be used in many ways in your solarpunk practice. They can be incorporated into spell bags, burned as incense, used in the creation of anointing oils, or simply placed on your altar to align your magickal workings with the Earth element. Remember to always source your herbs responsibly, prioritizing ethically harvested and organically grown herbs to align with solarpunk values of environmental responsibility and sustainability.

---

81 Another reminder that white sage specifically is a highly endangered plant, and that its use by those who aren't of Native American origin is cultural appropriation that Indigenous tribes have asked the pagan community to stop engaging in.

Earth-Associated Natural Oils

Essential oils serve as powerful tools in witchcraft, often used to enhance the magickal properties of rituals and spells, or simply to create a sacred space. Just as with herbs, certain essential oils correspond with the Earth element due to their grounding, nurturing, and stabilizing properties. Moreover, these essential oils are often derived from Earth-associated herbs, reinforcing the connection between the plant and its earthy energy. For these reasons, a ton of overlap can exist between lists of Earth-associated herbs and oils. Without being repetitive then, below are a few Earth-associated essential oils I've found particularly useful in my solarpunk craft practice. Of course, this list is by no means exhaustive. You can make an Earth-based essential oil infusion using any herb associated with the element of Earth or the Earth's energy in general.

Table 9 — Earthy Oil Infusions

Cypress	Known for its stabilizing properties, cypress essential oil can be used in solarpunk witchcraft when working on long-term sustainability projects that require endurance and steadfastness.
Sandalwood	Sandalwood is associated with grounding and connection. It's a good choice for solarpunk workings that aim to strengthen your connection to the Earth and the collective.
Myrrh	Myrrh, with its rich, resinous scent, has been used for grounding and protection for centuries. In the context of solarpunk witchcraft, myrrh can serve as a powerful protective ally against forces that threaten environmental and social health.

When using these essential oils in your solarpunk practice, consider adding them to a diffuser during rituals or spellwork, or mixing them into a carrier oil for anointing candles or yourself. As with herbs, always ensure you are sourcing your oils responsibly. Aim for suppliers that offer sustainably harvested and ethically produced essential oils to align with the solarpunk ethos of sustainability and social justice.

Remember, safety is paramount when working with essential oils. These oils are potent and should always be diluted before use. Some people may also have allergic reactions to certain oils, so always do a patch test before using a new oil. Also, some essential oils can be harmful if ingested or used improperly. Always use caution and do your research before incorporating a new essential oil into your practice.

Stones and Crystals Associated with the Element of Earth

Crystals and stones function as physical manifestations of Earth's energy, influencing our own energy. Esoteric thought and practice regarding the four classical elements can be traced back to ancient civilizations,[82] and they are just as relevant today in solarpunk witchcraft. Table 10 lists a few Earth-associated stones and crystals solarpunk witches can use in their practices:

Table 10 — Stones and Crystals Associated with the Element Earth

Moss Agate	Moss agate is a stabilizing stone strongly connected with nature. It's often used to rejuvenate your connection with Earth and can be utilized in solarpunk spells or rituals focused on environmental healing or sustainability.
Smoky Quartz	Known for its grounding and balancing properties, smoky quartz is an ideal stone for solarpunk witches working on creating balance in our ecosystems or in societal structures. It's also an excellent stone for absorbing and neutralizing negative energy, which can be particularly useful in activist spaces.

82 Michela Pereira. Alchemy, 1998, doi:10.4324/9780415249126-Q001-1. Routledge Encyclopedia of Philosophy, Taylor and Francis, rep.routledge.com/articles/thematic/alchemy/v-1.

Green Aventurine	Known as the stone of opportunity, green aventurine can help bring optimism and zest for life. Its connection to Earth makes it an excellent tool for any solarpunk work focused on creating a brighter and greener future.
Hematite	Hematite helps with grounding and protecting. It is also a stone of the mind, boosting memory and original thinking, making it a great companion for solarpunk witches strategizing creative and innovative solutions to environmental and societal issues.
Jasper	This grounding stone is known for its nurturing properties and connection to the Earth. It's excellent for absorbing negative energy and promoting environmental responsibility. Often associated with tranquility and wholeness, jasper encourages us to be honest with ourselves and to work harmoniously with others—concepts that align well with the solarpunk ethos. Different varieties of jasper (such as red jasper or picture jasper) may also bring additional properties into your practice, allowing you to fine-tune your connection with the Earth element.

To incorporate these stones and crystals into your solarpunk practice, you might place them on your Earth altar, use them to enhance the energy of a spell, carry them as a talisman during activist work, or meditate with them to attune your energy to the element of Earth. As with herbs and essential oils, please ensure you're sourcing your stones responsibly. Mining can have significant environmental and human rights implications, so do your research and choose suppliers who prioritize ethical and sustainable practices.

Remember, while these stones are associated with the element Earth, the practical fact is that all stones and crystals are directly from the Earth. That being the case, the most important aspect is your personal connection and intention. Feel free to use other stones or crystals that resonate with you and your personal solarpunk practice.

Earth Archetypes

In your solarpunk witchcraft practice, you might choose to work with certain deities or archetypes that embody the energy and qualities of the Earth element. These entities can serve as guides or mentors in your spiritual journey, helping you connect more deeply with the Earth and the solarpunk principles of sustainability and respect for the natural world. Table 11 below contains examples of Earth-related deity archetypes from a variety of world cultures and associated with both the masculine and the feminine.

Table 11 — Earth Deity Archetypes

Gaia	In Greek mythology, Gaia is the primordial goddess of the Earth, revered as the ancestral mother of all life. She embodies the living, breathing Earth and is associated with fertility, sustenance, and the interconnected web of life.
The Green Man	The Green Man is a symbol found in many cultures around the world, often representing rebirth and the cycle of growth each spring. As a representation of the spirit of nature itself, the Green Man can guide your understanding of the rhythms of the Earth and the importance of biodiversity.
Pachamama	In the Andean Indigenous cultures, Pachamama is a goddess revered as the Earth/time mother, but, in many ways, is genderfluid. She governs planting and harvesting and is also the embodiment of the mountains and causes earthquakes.

Geb	In ancient Egyptian mythology, Geb was the god of the Earth and one of the first gods to appear from the sea of chaos at the beginning of time. He's a central figure in the ancient Egyptian creation myth and is often depicted lying beneath the sky goddess Nut, his sister and wife.
Terra	In Roman mythology, Terra is the goddess of the Earth, equivalent to Gaia in the Greek pantheon. She embodies the terrestrial sphere and represents the inexhaustible life force of nature.
Papatūānuku	In Maori mythology from Aotearoa (New Zealand), Papatūānuku is an Earth. All life is born from her and returns to her upon death, and she is deeply respected and revered.
Nana Buluku	In West African Yoruba and Dahomey tradition, Nana Buluku is the supreme deity, the grandmother of all deities, often associated with the Earth and the moon.
Dagda	The Dagda is a father figure and protector of the Irish gods in Celtic mythology. He is associated with fertility, agriculture, manliness and strength, as well as magic, druidry, and wisdom.

If you choose to work with deities and archetypes from a culture you aren't part of, please be sure to read the note in the section on working with solar deities and archetypes on page 128.

EARTH MAGICK

In our quest to foster a sustainable, equitable, and vibrant future, solarpunk witchcraft—by its very nature—is intrinsically intertwined with the magick of the Earth. It is not merely about acknowledging Earth's presence in our rituals; it's about profoundly respecting and cherishing our relationship with the planet in all aspects of our lives, our Craft, and our activism. It's about understanding the Earth not just as a symbol, but as a living, breathing entity that is both the source and recipient of our magick.

Earth magick in solarpunk witchcraft is not an abstract concept; it's a tangible and critical part of our path. It encompasses not just the spells and rituals we perform but extends to our everyday actions and decisions: the food we eat, the energy we use, the products we buy, how we dispose of waste, and how we engage with our communities. Earth magick joins our magickal practice with the rhythms of nature and the goal of working towards the preservation and healing of our planet. This section will guide you in integrating Earth magick into your solarpunk witchcraft practice, helping you align your magickal journey with your commitment to a sustainable and equitable future.

Creating an Earth Altar

Altars serve as focal points for our magickal practice, embedding the sacred into our everyday experiences. As solarpunk witches, our primary commitment is to honor and safeguard our planet Earth, the life-giving entity that we inhabit. Having an Earth altar, alongside your main altar, is a poignant reminder of this commitment, further grounding your practice in the Earth's embrace.

To begin creating your Earth altar, choose a flat, undisturbed space in your home that can serve this purpose. Lay down an altar cloth on this surface, representing your intention to dedicate this space to Earth magick. The placement of your altar items is flexible and should align with your personal preference. For guidance on traditional placements of tools like the pentacle, elemental symbols, and deity candles, refer to pagan, Wiccan, or Craft primers, several of which are included in the appendix at the back of this book. However, the ultimate arrangement should resonate with your personal aesthetic and intuitive sense of order.

The following are a few suggestions for items emblematic of Earth and its energies. Remember, none of these are obligatory.

Select what resonates with you, what helps you forge a connection with the Earth and its nurturing, grounding energy.

Table 12 — Earth Altar Items

Altar Cloth	This could be any large enough cloth that embodies the spirit of Earth for you. Consider colors such as green or brown, or patterns that mimic the land or foliage.
Candles	Opt for candles that echo the Earth's colors—greens, browns, or even blues (to symbolize the planet's water bodies). Be sure to use soy or beeswax candles, not paraffin candles made with petroleum products.
Earth Symbols	Consider using images or items representing the Earth, such as small stones, crystals, or symbols of Earth deities/archetypes. You could even include a small globe or map.
Incense	Use incense made from a blend of herbs associated with the Earth (see page 157), or a diffuser with an essential oil that captures Earth's scent, such as patchouli or vetiver.
Plants or Seeds	Houseplants, succulents, flowers, or even bowls of seeds can symbolize growth and the fertility of the Earth.
Sand/Soil	A small jar or bowl of soil or sand is a direct representation of the Earth.
Other Natural Items	Consider adding found natural items, like leaves, feathers, pine cones, or seashells.

Remember, an Earth altar in solarpunk witchcraft is not just symbolic—it's a call to action. As you commune with your altar, let it inspire you towards practices that protect and heal our planet, such as conservation, sustainable living, and advocating for policies that protect our Earth. As solarpunk witches, our magick is rooted in the love of Earth, its bounty, and our duty to safeguard it for future generations.

Charging Ritual Tools with Earth Energy

Just like you can charge your tools with the power of the Moon or Sun (see Chapter Six), you can also charge your ritual tools with the power of the Earth. In this example, we'll charge an athame, or ritual knife used by witches, to cast a ritual circle.

Begin by preparing yourself and your space. Ensure that your athame is clean and that you are in a place where you can focus without being disturbed. You may choose to cast a circle, if that is part of your practice, or you may simply wish to cleanse the area by smudging with sage, ringing a bell, or any other method you prefer.

Next, sit or stand comfortably, and take a few deep, slow breaths to ground and center yourself. Hold your athame in your dominant hand, or both hands if you feel so guided, and close your eyes. Imagine roots sprouting from your feet and burrowing deep into the Earth. Feel the cool, stabilizing energy of the Earth rising through these roots, up through your body, and into your hands, and visualize this energy flowing into your athame, permeating it with the power and vitality of the Earth.

At your altar, take a pinch of salt and combine it with water in your chalice or a small bowl. Salt is a powerful symbol of the Earth, and water is an integral and vital part of planet Earth. Use your athame to stir the water and combine it with the salt. Dip your fingers into the salt water and sprinkle the blade and hilt of your athame while speaking your intention aloud, or in mind, by saying something like the following:

By the salt of the Earth
By the rivers and oceans of the Earth
By the power of the Earth
I bless and charge this athame.

that it may aid me in my work
for a sustainable and equitable future.
May it guide my magick with wisdom,
strength, and connection to the Earth.

Feel free to tailor this intention to suit your personal needs and the specific purpose you have for your athame. Then finally, thank the Earth for its energy and visualize the roots from your feet gently retracting, bringing your grounding visualization to a close. You may choose to leave your athame on your Earth altar (if you have one) for a full day and night to further absorb Earth energy, or you may choose to start working with it right away.

Remember, the key to successful charging of your athame, or any magickal tool, is your intention and focus. The energy of the Earth is a potent force that can greatly enhance your magick, especially when working towards solarpunk goals of environmental stewardship and social justice.

OTHER EARTH ENERGY SPELLWORK

Being the one of the four classical elements that we literally, physically inhabit and rely on for sustenance, the Earth symbolizes the very planet that solarpunk witchcraft aims to protect, nurture, and live in harmony with. With that in mind then, here are a variety of other ways solarpunk witches can weave Earth magick into their activism. This list is by no means exhaustive, and you should feel free to come up with your own meaningful ways to incorporate Earth magick into your solarpunk Craft practice.

Rituals for Ecological Healing

Incorporating Earth magick in rituals geared towards ecological healing and restoration can be immensely powerful. These rituals could involve burying biodegradable symbols of healing (such as seeds or eco-friendly charms) in the Earth, charging them with the intent of healing the Earth.

Working with Earth Deities/Archetypes

Petitioning Earth deities and archetypes in your spells and rituals can bring about stronger connections to the planet. Their wisdom and guidance can be invoked in order to seek solutions to environmental issues.

Protection Spells

Use Earth-associated herbs, crystals, or oils in protection spells for endangered species, threatened ecosystems, or environmental activists. Incorporate symbols that represent these into your spellwork.

Charging Tools and Symbols

Use Earth energy to charge the magickal tools and symbols you use in your activism. This could mean burying a protest sign or charm in the earth under a waxing moon, or placing Earth-associated crystals on top of a petition or map.

Plant Magick

Engage in plant magick, by growing your own herbs or trees and dedicating them to your environmental work.

Community Healing

Consider ways you can use Earth magick for community healing and justice. This could be as simple as planting and maintaining community gardens in urban food deserts, or leading community Earth-centered meditation or healing rituals in areas impacted by environmental racism.

Land Acknowledgment and Restoration Spell

Recognize the Indigenous history of the land you live on, and support Indigenous-led land stewardship initiatives. This can be part of Earth magick practice, acknowledging the spiritual sovereignty of Indigenous nations and their sacred relationship with the land. On page 222, you'll find an example of a land acknowledgment and restoration spell I've created and use often.

•   •   •

Earth Magick within the solarpunk witchcraft context emphasizes the connection and reverence for the Earth alongside powerful solar energies. In this chapter, we learned and practiced Earth-based meditations, spells, and correspondences that foster a sustainable and equitable future. We also worked through practical exercises for grounding, connecting with Earth's energies, and integrating Earth magick into solarpunk practices for personal empowerment and environmental activism. All this underlines the Earth's vital role in nurturing life and the importance of aligning magickal practices with ecological sustainability and respect for the planet.

Remember that, as with all magick, the key to Earth magick is your intent and focus. The physical actions you take in your rituals and spells are significant, but it's the mental and emotional energy you put into them that truly makes the magick happen. Incorporate Earth magick into your solarpunk witchcraft in ways that resonate with you and that align with your environmental and social justice goals.

Part Three:

Solarpunk Spellwork

*T*he third and final section of this book takes us head first into the realm of solarpunk magick. This is where we consciously make an active turn toward the external, toward the community, the ecosystem, and the planet. Why? Because self-improvement and inner spiritual evolution alone aren't enough if the world around us is burning. We practice an Earth- and nature-based spirituality. For that reason it's vital that our spiritual and magickal practice also serve the Earth and nature—that it serves our communities and our society.

The chapters of our solarpunk book of shadows that follow then take the practice of witchcraft and solar magick and situate them firmly within radical leftist ideology and political action in service of creating a better world and building the utopia we all dream of together as solarpunks. In these final four chapters, we outline a number of spells that can be used to fight climate change, heal the environment, protect animals, develop a relationship of harmony between humanity and nature, fight racism and patriarchy, and magickally engage in struggles against fascism, capitalism, and imperialism and for racial justice, gender justice, workers rights, and more.

In short, the following are solarpunk spells that can be used to demand utopia. But as stated in the introduction to this book, desire and intention and magickal work aren't sufficient by themselves when it comes to issues of such high stakes and global importance. For that reason, the spells in this section are accompanied by lists of practical, material actions you can take to reinforce your magick and manifest your spellwork in the physical world.

Chapter Eight: Spells to Fight Climate Change

*D*emanding utopia—adapting and finding solutions to climate change that lead to a better and more just world—is at the heart of the solarpunk movement. For that reason, we begin this section with a series of spells for fostering utopia by fighting climate change, its human causes, and its effects on our communities.

SPELL TO DEMAND UTOPIA

"Demand Utopia" is the slogan and call to action of the solarpunk community and movement. By struggling for justice, developing creative solutions to climate change, and fostering safe and resilient communities, we can pull ourselves out of the apocalyptic pit we've fallen into and create a high-tech, post-scarcity world of compassion and harmony with nature. The first spell in this chapter, then, is a spell to demand utopia.

Supplies:
- Small hand drum
- Chant sheets

Prepare for and perform the basic solarpunk ritual outlined in Chapter Four. When you get to Step 9 of the ritual on page 75, perform the following musical, chant-based spell. If you're doing the spell solitary, then pick up the drum. If you're performing group magick, decide who will be the drummer. The drummer will keep a 4/4 beat at 140 BPM. Put more simply, hit the drum in even intervals of about one beat every half second.[83] The fast pace of the drum beat combined with the chanting helps build and increase the strength of the cone of power.

---

83 You can find an audio example of a 4/4 beat at 140 BPM at youtube.com/watch?v=J6T03zYnKUQ.

After the drummer begins the beat, repeat the following chant. If you're doing the spell solitary, you can ignore the parts in parentheses and just hit the drum one beat for each word in the parentheses before moving onto the next line. If you're doing group magic, have one person say the parts not in parentheses and the rest of the group chant the parts in parentheses together as a call and response.

I will a thing (We see a thing)
A thing for we (A thing for we)
I will a thing (We will a thing)
A thing to be (A thing to be)

A better world (A better world)
That's just and fair (That's just and fair)
Compassion rules (Compassion rules)
And we all share (And we all share)

We hereby end (We hereby end)
Dystopia (Dystopia)
Now we demand (Now we demand)
Utopia (Utopia)

This is the thing (This is the thing)
That I do see (That I do see)
This is the thing (This is the thing)
I will to be (We will to be)

On the last word of the chant, the drummer hits the drum extra hard for emphasis and then abruptly stops. The silent power of magick fills the sacred circle. You can feel the air crackling with the power of Earth and Sun. Sit in silence and allow the inspiration spirit of the spellwork move through you. Allow that inspiration to form words and images in your mind's eye of what utopia looks like and feels like. If the spirit moves you, allow it to speak through by saying out loud things that contribute to a better world. Examples of things participants might say include, but aren't limited to the following:

- Racial and gender justice
- Universal healthcare
- Plenty for all
- Homes for all
- Equitable distribution
- An end to fossil fuel consumption
- Harmony with Nature

Once you've given the group plenty of time to share, finish out the basic solarpunk ritual and close the circle.

Spellwork Praxis
Reinforce your magick and help manifest your spellwork in the physical world by any of the following:

- doing volunteer work with a mutual aid group or radical movement organization,
- engaging in political education around social justice and system change,
- or helping and giving to someone in need.

SPELL TO PROTECT YOUR HOME FROM CLIMATE DISASTERS
From storms with strong winds and floods to heatwaves, wildfires, and unseasonal snow storms and freezing weather, climate disasters and emergencies are an increasingly regular and normal part of life around the world, and we continue to burn fossil fuels and drive climate change. The following spell then is to help protect your home from being ravaged by climate disaster. This spell can also

be modified for more broad community protection. Simply take the ingredients to the four directional quarters of your community, instead of your own individual home, and perform the smudging and sprinkling in each quarter to create a circle of protection around your community.

Mix any combination of the following with some sea salt.

- Ashwood
- Bay leaf
- Angelica herb
- Carnation flowers
- Clove
- Elmwood
- Garlic
- Mugwort (strengthens spells)
- Pine needles
- Sandalwood
- Sea salt
- Vervain (strengthens other herbs)

Grind your blend into a powder using a pestle and mortar. Then burn the blend as incense in every corner of your home (or whatever space you're protecting). From the inside, burn the incense along doorways that lead inside, along the windows, and along other entrance ways. Then go outside and move around the space deosil three times with your magickal blend burning. While performing the smudging, visualize a spherical shield of powerful light and energy beginning to surround your home, and recite words such as:

By the powers of Fire and Air,
This home is protected, I declare.
So mote it be.

Next, use your athame to mix salt into a bowl of water. Sprinkle the salt water in every corner of your home, along the doorway, and along the windows. Move around your house deosil three times, sprinkling the salt water as you go. While performing the spell, continue visualizing the protective shield forming and strengthening around your home. Recite words such as,

By the powers of Earth and Sea,
This home is safe.
So mote it be.

Spellwork Praxis

After doing this spell to protect your own space from the worsening effects of climate change, take action in the physical world by doing the following:

- Create a concrete evacuation plan for you and your family in case you need to leave for your safety.
- Take practical steps to protect your home from extreme weather events by doing things such as
  - keeping weeds and brush trimmed around your home,
  - cleaning rain gutters,
  - or using caulk to seal cracks or leaks that could let water into your home.
- Volunteer at a cold weather shelter during the winter.
- Do research into what communities are the most affected by the changing climate. Find out how you can support them in efforts to adapt to and combat those effects. Then choose how to take action and get to work.
- Spend time volunteering with Habitat for Humanity or a similar organization in your area that builds tiny houses or other homes for those in need so everyone has a roof and walls to protect them from weather events.

SPELL TO CALM THE WINDS AND WAVES

The following spell can be used or modified to calm winds and waves when a hurricane or big storm is on the horizon. The spell can easily be modified to apply to rivers, flash floods, and similar weather events by appropriately altering the language and visualizations used during the spell.

Supplies:
- Sun water
- Salt
- A jar with a lid
- A shovel

When you arrive at Step 9 of the basic solarpunk ritual (page 75), move to your altar and use your athame to add three scoops of salt to the jar. Then, with the jar and a bowl or glass of water, move around the circle to the western quarter and the element of water. Face the pentagram you drew earlier as a gateway for the spirits and representations of water (see Step 5 of the basic solarpunk ritual on page 71-72), and pour the water into the jar.

While doing so, visualize the raging ocean being contained, just as the water is contained by the jar. While pouring and visualizing, say the following or something similar of your own creation:

> *Powers of Water, I beseech thee,*
> *Still the mighty, raging sea.*
>
> *So mote it be.*

Next, move around the circle to the southern quarter (or the eastern, depending on your tradition or preference) and the element of Air. Face the pentagram you drew earlier in Step 5 (see page 72) as a gateway for the spirits and representations of Air, and blow into the open jar of salt water and put on the lid.

While doing so, visualize the raging winds being contained, just as the wind created by your breath is now contained by the jar. While blowing, visualizing, and containing the air along with the water, say the following or something similar of your own creation:

> *Powers of Air, I beseech thee, hail,*
> *Still the mighty, raging gale.*
>
> *So mote it be.*

Finally, use a shovel to bury the jar in your yard, near the edge of your community, or keep it covered in a dark, quiet place (like the back of a closet) where it can remain undisturbed until the threat of a hurricane or similar climate disaster has passed.

Spellwork Praxis

In addition to performing the above spell, you can do any of the following work to reinforce the energy and power of your magick:

- Volunteer at an evacuation shelter during the rainy season, especially if you aren't in an evacuation zone.

- Go online and look into which islands and coastal cities are at risk of being the first destroyed by rising sea levels,[84] or which communities are most at risk from the increasing strength of hurricanes and cyclones.

- Make a banner and hang it over a highway bridge, or hold it on a busy street corner during rush hour to raise awareness of people's plight in places like Jakarta, Bangkok, and Mumbai.

- Find community organizations in your area run by and for those who are most at risk, and support those organizations by volunteering, donating, or otherwise contributing to their work.

SPELL TO BRING RAIN TO SNUFF OUT WILDFIRES

Spells, prayers, dances, and other magickal work to bring much-needed rain aren't a new practice; they weren't born out of the modern realities and concerns associated with human-induced climate change. Here on the North American continent, such practices go back centuries at least. Rainmaking through dance and other rituals was common among Indigenous tribes, particularly in

---

84 Here is one potential resource: greenroofs.com/2022/03/02/these-36-world-cities-will-be-underwater-first.

the dry desert region of the stolen land referred to as the southwest United States.

The following two spells aren't taken from western Indigenous culture and practices. Solarpunk is decidedly not about creating racist stereotypes, nor is it about cultural appropriation. I'm not Indigenous to this land. My family comes from a long line of European immigrant, settler colonizers who invaded and stole this land. For those who either aren't Indigenous, or those who are but want to experiment and expand your book of shadows, the following is a spell I created using water magick to encourage water to fall from the skies.

Living where I do in the U.S. Pacific Northwest, wildfires have become an annual scourge as a result of climate change, and they are only getting worse. We aren't the only region experiencing this increase in fire activity either. I do this spell fairly often during fire season, especially since I live in a rural and forested area.

Supplies:
- Sun water
- A cauldron or firepit
- Fire starting materials

When you arrive at Step 9 of the basic solarpunk ritual during which magickal work is performed (see page 75 for reference), start a small fire in your cauldron before raising a cone of power. If your cauldron is large enough, you can start a small wood fire. Another option is to put a candle in the center of the cauldron and light the candle.

Once the first is going, raise a cone of power by visualizing a funnel of water forming on the ground, circling around you, and rising up into the sky and falling back down on the fire in the form of rain. When you feel the energy is at a peak, say something like:

Powers of Water, healing rains, I call you. Come and Snuff out the flames that threaten our community.

So mote it be.

As you say, "So mote it be," use the water to douse the flames in the cauldron.

Spellwork Praxis

Reinforce your spellwork by gathering with others in your community to form mutual aid groups and networks.[85] Such networks can

- volunteer at an evacuation shelter during wildfire season, especially if you aren't in an evacuation zone,

- respond locally and quickly to help each other and the rest of the community when threatened by wildfires or other climate disasters,

- develop emergency resource distribution plans that can be rapidly implemented to help community members in need,

- and help undercut disaster capitalists who seek to take advantage of people and profit from emergencies and community distress.

SPELL TO END A DROUGHT

Drought conditions have become all too common across the world as a result of human induced climate change. This problem not only exacerbates wildfires, but threatens freshwater supplies we use for drinking water and other purposes. Desert cities such as Las Vegas, which perhaps should never have been built in the first place, face severe risk. Lake Mead, which is the reservoir that provides Vegas with its water, is rapidly drying out.[86] The following spell then, is designed to put energy and power toward droughts ending.

Supplies:

---

85 Scott Crow's book, *Black Flags and Windmills: Hope, Anarchy, and the Common Ground Collective*, is a great resource to start learning more about organizing mutual aid networks, particularly in the context of community need following natural disasters.
86 You can learn more on the situation at Lake Mead here: a-z-animals.com/blog/why-is-lake-mead-drying-up-here-are-the-top-3-reasons

- Water (use moderation and don't be wasteful, especially if you're in an area that's currently experiencing a drought)

- A watering can, ideally one with a showerhead-like mouth on the spout, to most accurately mimic rain.

- Soil

- A large, deep bowl or a small bucket in which to combine the soil and water.[87]

If you're using a pot or bucket and soil, then fill up the container about half full. Less is perfectly fine too, depending on how much soil or dirt you have access to and depending on how big your bucket is. Fill the watering can with a base layer of water. It doesn't have to be a lot, especially if you're in a region experiencing drought.

Next, fill a small bowl about halfway with water and place it on top of the pentagram on your altar. If you don't have a pentagram or an altar, that's perfectly fine. Setting it on any flat surface will do. Your intention is more important than your accouterments.

Take a few deep, intentional breaths. Add to the bowl some herbs that have magickal correspondence to abundance and to the element of water. For abundance you could add hollyhock or dandelion.[88] Lily, aloe, jasmin, and willow are just a few of the numerous herbs that correspond with the element of water.[89] If you'd like, you can say some spell casting words as you add the herbs. For example:

With these herbs of abundance and Water

I add to the power of this spell.

---

87 Instead of a bucket and planting soil, you can also just use the Earth itself if you live in or can get to a place where that's possible.

88 Note: To my knowledge, dandelions aren't traditionally associated with abundance. However, they grow and spread in great abundance, and so, for me, the correspondence has always been both real and powerful. Always feel free to create your own associations and correspondences that make sense to you. You're under no obligation to consult other people's correspondence lists in order for your spell to be effective. Like the kitchen witch, it's also perfectly okay to simply use what you have available to you.

89 The following is a good starting place for a deeper dive into plants and herbs associated with water: groveandgrotto.com/blogs/articles/38875137-what-plants-and-herbs-are-attributed-to-water.

Next add some essential oil to the bowl of water. Orange, frankincense, patchouli, clove, ginger, myrrh, cinnamon bark, and spruce oils are all examples that correspond with abundance. For correspondence with the element of water, I've always thought of all essential oils being associated with that element due to their liquid form.

If you want to be more specific than that, any essential oil made from a plant associated with the element of water will share that association. For example, jasmine is on the above short list of herbs associated with water, so you could use jasmine oil as well, or you could use something different to add more variety. Other examples include lemon, bergamot, and sandalwood oils. Take deep breaths as you add the ingredients to the bowl. Focus on your intention. Say some spell casting words if you'd like:

> *With these magickal oils, I infuse*
> *this spell with the power of abundance.*
> *Blessed Be.*

Another item you could add to the bowl of water is semi-precious stones or crystals associated with the goal of the spell. For example, aquamarine is a water-associated stone (perhaps for obvious reasons). Green quartz is an example of one of the many crystals commonly associated with abundance.[90] Before placing the stones in the bowl, you can close your eyes, take some breaths, and visualize the stones being charged with the power of your intention. Then, as with the herbs and oils, you can say some words such as:

> *With the magickal power of these stones,*
> *I infuse this water with strength and abundance.*
> *Blessed Be.*

---

90 One of many resources on crystals associated with the idea of abundance is tinyrituals.co/blogs/tiny-rituals/crystals-for-prosperity.

Take your athame and hold it with both hands at head height up above the bowl. Close your eyes and again take a deep breath. See and feel the energy of your cone of power, the light of the Sun, and the lifeforce of the Earth, flowing through you and into your athame. Bring the magickal blade down slowly into the bowl of water and stir three times deosil, while chanting:

Rain for crops
Rain for thirst
Rain for life

Take the bowl of water from the altar and pour it into the watering can. Then, take the watering can over to the bucket of soil or to the spot of dirt outside that you've chosen. Again, close your eyes, then meditate and visualize the water in the can filling with the Sun- and Earth-made cone of power.

Begin pouring the water into the dry soil, symbolically giving new life to a parched patch of Earth. In your mind, see water falling from the sky and the newly wet Earth welcoming the rain with open arms. As you do so, continue infusing the visualization and your spell with the energy from your cone of power. As you pour, repeat the following or something similar:

By the element of Water and powers of creation, I cast this spell
and call on the rains to form and fall upon this land,
to feed our crops, to quench our thirst,
to bring new life to the Earth.
So mote it be.

Spellwork Praxis

Individual behavioral changes are no replacement for systemic solutions when it comes to fighting climate change and building a better world. But there's also room for individual growth and change. Solarpunk witches can take the following concrete actions around drought resistance and adaptation:

- Engage in campaigns and struggles around clean water issues. Ideas include, but aren't limited to
  - protesting or taking other action against fossil fuel companies and other corporations that pollute waterways,
  - getting involved in campaigns for tougher clean water regulations,
  - or working to hold city and school officials accountable for lead pipes in school plumbing systems.
- If you have a yard, remove your lawn and plant native plants, or utilize drought-resistant landscaping that uses rocks and desert plants such as beautifully flowering cacti and succulents.
- If you live in an area prone to drought or currently experiencing drought, or even if you live somewhere where rain is plentiful, research and implement ways you can be more responsible with your water use.

SPELL TO EXPOSE THE CRIMES OF FOSSIL FUEL COMPANIES AND EXECUTIVES[91]

This spell can be performed when you want to expose the corruption, backroom manipulation, and crimes of fossil fuel corporations and their executives (or for that matter, any corporation). This is an example of a spell that is carried out over the course of several days. Ideally, begin day one during a waning moon.

Supplies:
- One onion
- Boline or kitchen knife
- A pin or needle long enough to stick into the center of the onion

Start by taking an onion and cutting off the top. Dress the onion with solar water and essential oil the way you would a candle. Next,

91 This spell was inspired by a commonly known spell to reveal hidden truths. Another, much more basic example of this widely practiced and passed down magickal spell can be found at Llewellyn's blog: llewellyn.com/spell.php?spell_id=7630.

place the onion on a flat surface, and while holding the outside of the onion firmly with one hand, stick a needle all the way into the onion's core. The top of the needle should be inside of or flush with the outside layer of the onion. The pin represents the truth that's being concealed by the corporation and their executives.

The next step is to sit with the onion in your hands. Focus on your intention: exposing the crimes of fossil fuel empires. Visualize such crimes coming to light. See the public's reaction of outrage. See the world taking action in support of justice for those crimes being served. Build up your will, your desire, your energetic power as you do this visualization. Then, imbue the onion with that intention, that visualization, that power.

After you've filled the onion with your magickal intention, the next step is to peel the first, top layer off the onion. As you peel, visualize a barrier cracking and breaking, and the truth being hidden by the corporation getting closer and closer to being revealed. Each subsequent night, ideally at the same time each night, peel off the next layer of the onion while doing the visualization. Continue this each night until you reach the pin at the center. While peeling the last layer and revealing the pin, visualize the barrier finally and completely cracking, and truth being revealed.

Spellwork Praxis
There are a number of ways you can put this spell into practice:
- Use your social media pages to share information about the crimes of fossil fuel companies and their executives.[92]
- Make graphics or gifs to share about exposed fossil fuel company crimes.
- Volunteer with or otherwise support an organization that works with and supports whistleblowers.[93]

---

92 It's important to make sure information you spread is accurate and not rooted in conspiracy theories. Conspiracy theories have dangerous consequences and are often rooted in anti-Semitic tropes.
93 Here's one list of organizations that provide resources and support for whistleblowers: spj.org/whistleblower/whistleblowing-organizations.asp.

- Organize or attend protests against fossil fuel companies and executives. In addition, organize or attend rallies in support of clean and renewable energy.

SPELL TO BANKRUPT FOSSIL FUEL COMPANIES

Fossil fuel companies are the primary cause of climate change. Other institutions such as the U.S. military[94] are also giant culprits, but through their use of the resources sold to them by fossil fuel companies. Fossil fuel companies have also helped significantly slow the progress of alternative, clean, and renewable energy development. If we're going to stop climate change before it's too late, if we're going to build utopia, then we need to end the widespread global use of fossil fuels. That means putting fossil fuel companies out of business.

Supplies:
- Cauldron
- Lighter or matches
- Other fire-starting materials like wood, newspaper, or candles
- Marker or pen
- Fake money of any denomination as a symbolic representation
- Water (for safety)

When you arrive at the point in the basic solarpunk ritual during which magickal work is performed, do the following spell:

Start a small wood or candle fire in your cauldron. Once the fire is going, move to the altar and using the marker or pen, write the names of fossil fuel companies on the fake money. You can also

---

94 Neta C. Crawford's recent book, *The Pentagon, Climate Change, and War: Charting the Rise and Fall of US Military Emissions*, shows that the U.S. military is the largest fossil fuel users among all U.S. governmental institutions, emitting about 51 million metric tons of CO_2 emissions per year in 2020 and 2021: motherjones.com/environment/2022/10/pentagon-climate-change-neta-crawford-book.

draw symbols to represent the companies instead of or in addition to writing their names.

Then, take the fake money over to the cauldron (if it isn't on top of your altar). Hold the fake money over the cauldron and visualize the bankruptcy and financial ruin of the fossil fuel companies. Draw energy from your cone of power into your visualization and imbue the fake money with that power. When you're ready, burn the fake money in the cauldron fire and repeat the following:

By the element of Fire, power of destruction and creation
I manifest this spell to protect the Earth.
So mote it be.

Spellwork Praxis

In addition to your magickal work, the following practical work will help manifest your spell in the physical world:

- Research what fossil fuel–related businesses are in your area. It could be fossil fuel transport companies, companies that manufacture parts or machines for fossil fuel companies, gas stations owned by multinational fossil fuel companies, among other possible kinds of businesses.
- Organize (or attend) a protest or direct action against a local fossil fuel company, especially if there are any known to be particularly harmful to the community.
- Join or organize divestment campaigns to get local governments in your area to pull their investments out of fossil fuel companies and mutual funds that include such companies.
- Brainstorm ways the community can come together to disrupt fossil fuel company operations and cost them money. For example:
  - filing lawsuits or injunctions,
  - organizing community pickets,

- or disrupting events sponsored by fossil fuel companies and/or attended by their executives and other representatives.

SPELL FOR ADVANCES IN RENEWABLE ENERGY TECHNOLOGY

It's not enough to simply end fossil fuels. Without an adequate replacement supply of clean and renewable energy, we run the distinct risk of sliding into an eco-primitivist, fascist nightmare. In that spirit, the following spell uses sigil magick to encourage advances in renewable energy technology.

Supplies:
- Pen or pencil
- Parchment paper
- A match or lighter

As discussed in Chapter Six, a sigil is a pictorial representation of the desire you want to manifest. Often, they include runes and other magickal symbols, but that's by no means necessary. Generally, when a sigil is drawn or created in some other way, it's imbued with intention and power and then burned to activate and release the spell.

The sigil I've created as a spell for advances in renewable energy technology is below. Feel free to use it, modify it, or create your own entirely new sigil.

Clean energy tech sigil (by Justine Norton-Kertson)

Once you've imbued the sigil with your intention and energy from the cone of power you raised, burn the sigil in the fire to activate it. If you'd like, as it burns, you can say things such as:

By the forces of Nature, the Sun, the Moon, and the Earth
I activate and release this spell with the Power of Fire
So mote it be

As it continues burning, visualize the magick of the sigil and your intention being released into the world to manifest. (Spellwork praxis for this spell will be included in the praxis for the following spell.)

SPELL TO INCREASE RENEWABLE ENERGY PRODUCTION

Building a more utopian world means finding ways to produce large amounts of energy without fossil fuels and other drivers of climate change and global pollution. The following spell is meant to help infuse that reality with the power of intention and manifesting, to inspire your action in making that vision come to pass.

Jar spells have a long history, going back at least three hundred years.[95] Centuries ago, this kind of spell was used as a kind of counter-magic to protect against curses and hexes. Nowadays, jar spells are used for a virtually boundless range of purposes.

Supplies:
- A jar with lid
- Herbs
- Crystals and other magickal stones
- Sun water
- Any images or objects that represent renewable energy to you

---

95 Joseph Glanvill (1700), *Saducismus Triumphatus: or, Full and Plain Evidence Concerning Witches and Apparitions*, page 109, 3rd edition, A. L., London (archive.org/details/saducismustriump00glan).

To perform a jar spell, you'll need a jar with a lid. The jar should be big enough to fit the items with which you plan to fill it. You'll also need a candle and whatever items you want in your jar.

You can fill the jar with any items you want. But it makes sense to find and use objects that in some way symbolically represent the work you're doing. In this case, items that represent increase and abundance—as well as items that represent energy, energy production, technology, invention, creation, and newness—would all be appropriate. You might also add items that represent the Sun, the wind, or other natural resources that can be used to produce clean energy.

You might add an abundance herb like hollyhock to your jar. Or maybe echinacea, often used by witches to add strength to abundance spells. Energy could be represented by a battery, a small power chord, or even by a plant or leaves (think photosynthesis, the process plants use to turn sunlight, water, and carbon dioxide into fuel).[96] Technology, like energy, could be represented by something like a power cord or battery or some old car fuses.

In order to represent the concept of invention, creation, and newness, you can add sprigs of chervil to your jar. Also known as french parsley, this herb corresponds magickally to—among other things—bringing in new life, such as the life of a new technology. You can put sunstones and cinnamon in your jar to represent solar power. You can also use sunflower seeds to represent both the Sun and new life/creation. Feathers could represent the air and wind. Finally, you can also think of something to put in the jar as a representation of currently unknown, future renewable energy technologies.

Of course, you can choose items completely different from these. What's most important is that for you, the items represent the intention of increasing global renewable energy production.

---

96 If you're interested in learning more about photosynthesis, a good starting place is this educational resource from *National Geographic*: education.nationalgeographic.org/resource/photosynthesis

As you place items in the jar, hold them in your hands and visualize your intention and fill the items with that power. You can carve or write sigils onto some of the items, anoint them with essential oils associated with creation and abundance, and do other similar things to increase the intention within the jar. If you'd like, you can also add some words to your spell as you place each item in your jar, when you've put the last item in the jar, or as you seal the jar. For example, you could say,

By adding this (item's name),
I declare a renewable energy future.
So mote it be.

When you finish adding items to your jar, add the lid. Now it's time to seal the jar. This is where the candle comes in handy. Light the candle and use the melted wax to create a seal around the lid of the jar. Let the remainder of the candle burn while you meditate on your spell, visualize a utopian renewable energy future, and continue infusing the jar with the energy from your cone of power, your visualization, and your passionate intention and desire.

After the candle burns out, you can decorate your jar if you'd like, but this is by no means required. Once you've finished, put the jar on your altar, or somewhere else that is both safe and important to you. If you ever want to recharge the spell, you can repeat the spell meditation and use another candle to drip more wax.

Spellwork Praxis

By taking any of the following concrete actions, you can work in the physical world to bolster the two clean, renewable energy spells outlined above:

- Find and support local and regional initiatives for new clean and renewable energy infrastructure.
- Get involved in campaigns to limit or tax fossil fuels.

- Use alternative sources of fuel and energy whenever possible.[97]
- Go online and research DIY methods of creating your own alternative energy at home and in your community.
  - If you're inclined toward building and mechanics, can you figure out ways to improve upon what you learn to make DIY energy production methods more efficient?
- Do research on how to identify and combat misinformation about fossil fuels and about renewable energy sources.

SPELL TO STOP PIPELINE CONSTRUCTION

From Standing Rock and Keystone XL in South Dakota to Jordan Cove in Oregon, stopping pipeline construction has become one of the frontlines in the fight to end fossil fuel use. Pipelines are often designed to run through Indigenous treaty lands in order to avoid colonial towns and cities. This has made the struggle against pipeline construction frontline in the battle for Indigenous sovereignty and to end imperialism.

In addition to protests, letter writing, and joining calls from Indigenous communities to join them on the front lines, the following spell can be used in the fight against new pipeline construction.

Supplies:

- Used, thin plastic
- Scissors

To perform this spell, you'll need at least two things: used plastic and scissors. I strongly discourage anyone from going out and buying plastic to use. But if you purchase anything that has plastic bags or sheets, bubble wrap, or other plastic packaging, you can save until you have enough to tie together into a one to three foot rope. Additional optional materials include duct tape or some other kind of tape, a sharpie pen, and paper.

---

97 While it's important to keep in mind the necessity of systemic solutions and their primary importance over and above individual, piecemeal solutions, as individuals, we can still take action and do things in our own lives to "be part of the solution."

Start by twisting up two pieces of plastic and connecting them by tying two ends together in a knot. Continue adding lengths of plastic in the same way until your rope is a couple feet long. The length of the "rope" itself represents the pipeline, and the plastic material represents the crude oil that flows through pipelines.

Next, tear off a strip of duct tape and wrap it around the center of your rope. Then, use the sharpie pen to write the name of the pipeline on the duct tape. If you don't have duct tape, you can wrap a piece of paper around the center of your rope and use any kind of tape to fasten it securely to the rope. Then, write the name of the pipeline on the paper. While creating your rope, focus on channeling your intention and energy from your cone of power into the rope.

Once you feel ready, take the rope and place it on the pentagram on your altar. Use your athame to dish salt in your water bowl and light incense. Use the water and incense to further charge your pipeline representation. While doing so, say something like:

By Salt and Sea,
I declare a world that's fossil fuel free.
So mote it be.

By Fire and Air,
An end to pipelines I declare.
So mote it be.

Finally, take the rope in your hands and pick up the scissors. Visualize the specific pipeline whose name is written on the rope. See it failing to be built. If construction has already started, see it somehow ending in a way you feel comfortable with. As you visualize, build energy from the Earth and your cone of power into your body, using yourself as a conduit to channel that energy into the rope, along with your desire and intention.

When you feel the energy reach a peak, use the scissors to cut the rope right down the center through the name of the pipeline. Sever the rope completely, symbolically ending the pipeline.

Spellwork Praxis

Work to bolster the above spell by taking any of the following concrete actions:

- Research the history of western colonization of Indigenous lands, invasions of tribal territory, and treaty violations to better understand the context of contemporary struggles over pipelines on Indigenous peoples' lands.

- Find Indigenous blockades and other efforts underway to stop pipeline construction in their territory. Aid their effort by sending money, supplies, and other resources. If Indigenous organizers have called for others to do so— consider joining them on the frontlines and putting your body and freedom on the line to defend Indigenous land from fossil fuel corporations.

SPELL TO STOP TAR SANDS EXTRACTION

Oil extracted from tar sands is even worse than the usual crude oil. In fact, tar sands oil extraction is often called a "carbon bomb," because of how bad it is for the environment and climate change. The extraction and processing of tar sands is much more energy intensive, using three times more energy to turn into useful fuel than conventional crude oil.[98] The movement of tar sands is also closely related to pipeline construction, which often purposely cuts through Indigenous treaty lands and endangers their communities in order to avoid colonial towns and cities. Tar sands have even been linked to higher cancer rates in Indigenous communities.[99]

98 The Center for Biological Diversity is a good starting place for those interested in learning more about the harms of the tar sands extraction process:biologicaldiversity. org/campaigns/no_tar_sands/index.html.

99 For more coverage of tar sands and higher cancer rates in Indigenous communities, see this article from the *Financial Post*: financialpost.com/news/oil-sands-pollution-linked-to-higher-cancer-rates-in-fort-chipewyan-study-finds.

The following spell can be used in the spirit of ending tar sands extraction.

Supplies:
- Small glass jar
- Small spoon that will fit through the mouth of the jar
- Hand towel
- Candle
- Sand (soil or dirt will do fine if you can't obtain sand)
- Molasses

Fill your jar about halfway with sand, and fill it with molasses until the jar is about three quarters of the way full. Use the spoon to stir the molasses and sand together. Using your fingers, keep the sand and molasses in the jar as you pull the spoon out of the jar. It will be sticky and may take a minute. Stay relaxed and don't let it frustrate you.

Once you've mixed together the contents of your jar, put the lid on it and use your candle to drip wax over the lid and seal the jar. Take your jar into your yard or somewhere you can bury it as a symbolic representation of the #KeepItInTheGround movement against fossil fuels. As you bury the jar, visualize the end of tar sands extraction and see tar sands deep underground, staying there where they belong.

Spellwork Praxis

There are struggles taking place across the U.S. to stop the transportation of tar sands coming out of Alberta, Canada. Often the bitumen[100] is being carried by train to a coastal port for processing and/or global distribution. You can support such efforts in a variety of ways:

- Support organizations such as Greenpeace and Ruckus that organize blockades or train activists in blockade techniques.

---

100 Bitumen is thick, black, sticky, residue that is a byproduct of the petroleum distillation process. It's commonly used for road surfacing and roofing applications.

- Find active tar sands transport blockades and support them by
  - sending supplies, money, or other resources to blockade camps,
  - donating to jail support and bail funds for those arrested during blockade actions,
  - or physically joining blockades yourself, if you're able to.

SPELL TO END COAL MINING

While all fossil fuels contribute to climate change and need to be reduced or eliminated from use, burning coal is worse for the environment than using either crude oil or natural gas.[101] The fight to prevent mountain removal and end coal use in general is nothing new. Important strides have been made and victories have been won,[102] but the struggle to end extractive coal mining and the burning of coal for electricity and heat production is by no means over.

You can easily use the above tar sands spell and substitute a lump of coal for the sand and molasses. Alternatively, you can take the lump of coal and set it on top of the pentagram on your altar. Visualize the end of coal mining, and imbue the combined energy of your vision for the future and your cone of power, then channel that energy into the lump of coal. When you feel the energy has reached a peak, put the lump of coal on the ground (taking it outside might be a good idea) and smash it to pieces with a hammer, symbolically shattering and ending the coal mining industry.

If you'd like, while smashing the coal, recite the following or similar words:

---

101 For more details on this topic, see this resource from *Our World in Data*: ourworldindata.org/safest-sources-of-energy#:~:text=We%20see%20this%20 from%20the,and%20renewables%20on%20both%20counts.
102 An example of such victories is a 2013 court ruling affirming the EPA's power under the Clean Water Act to veto mountain top removal projects like the Spruce Mine: grist.org/article/two-more-victories-in-the-fight-against-mountaintop-removal-coal-mining, and

Coal is dirty and pollutes the air.
End coal mining everywhere.
So mote it be.

Sweep up the pieces and bury them.

Spellwork Praxis

The suggestions above for stopping pipeline construction and tar sands extraction are also great for supporting practical efforts to end coal mining. When it comes down to it, all three sources of fossil fuels require violent extraction methods that damage the planet. All three also use similar methods of resource transport, particularly trains, long haul trucks, and overseas shipping vessels.

Another thing you can do to bolster your magick for all three is to find and support efforts for a Just Transition[103] away from fossil fuels. Such efforts work to place focus on those most affected by the transition, and ensure that the miners, oil rig workers, tar sands field workers, and other people who will lose their jobs during the transition away from fossil fuels receive the training they need to find living wage work in other industries that don't damage the planet.

SPELL TO COOL THE EARTH

Heat waves are an increasingly frequent and deadly consequence of climate change.[104] This is the case even in places like here in Oregon's Willamette Valley. When we first moved here almost two decades ago, Summer was mild. Temperatures generally ranged between the high seventies and high eighties. Every now and again,

---

103 Just Transition is the idea that healthy economies can coexist with a clean environment, and that the process for accomplishing this goal shouldn't come at the expense of workers' and community members' health and ability to find meaningful, living wage work. You can learn more about the Just Transition framework at climatejusticealliance.org/just-transition.

104 You can start learning more about heat waves and their connection to climate change by checking out this resource from the Center for Climate and Energy Solutions: c2es.org/content/heat-waves-and-climate-change.

it would break into the nineties, and for about a week per Summer, usually in late July or August, we'd experience temperatures in the high nineties. Rarely did we see three-digit temperatures, and if we did, it was generally for only a day.

Now, summertime is generally and noticeably hotter. Temperatures in the high seventies are more rare. High eighties and low nineties are much more normal. As I write this, we're moving into our third week of mid to high ninety-degree weather, and we'll have our first hundred-plus degree days. We aren't even halfway through the Summer yet.

In order to help provide relief during dangerous heat waves, you can perform or adapt the following spell, or use it as inspiration to create your own.

Supplies:
- A hand fan, or a piece of paper, cardboard, or similar material that can be used as a fan
- Pencil, pen, paint, or markers

When the time comes in your ritual to perform your spellwork, take your fan in hand. If you want one for each hand, that's perfectly fine as well. Close your eyes and take a few deep breaths to move further into a state of relaxation and trance.

Visualize yourself standing on a hill, also holding a fan or fans and overlooking your city, town, or the area experiencing a heat wave. As you look down on the places and people below, hold your fan or fans up above your head (both the fans in your actual hands and the ones you're visualizing in your mind's eye) and use them to begin generating a cool breeze around you.

See that breeze descend upon the land below and provide relief to the people, animals, and plants who live there. Feel the energy from your cone of power and the desire within you flowing into your visualization with the magickal force of will. Infuse your visualization with the power of radical hope. Repeat the following words, or something similar:

By the powers of Air,
Wind, gust, breeze, and gale,
Cool, refreshing breath of Nature
Blow upon this land.

(repeat the above lines three times, then say)

So mote it be.

You're more than welcome to incorporate ecstatic dance into this spell as well. You can easily do so by dancing in addition to waving your fans to generate a breeze.

Spellwork Praxis

There are a variety of practical steps and actions you can take in order to help manifest this spell. As with the "Spell to End Coal Mining" we just went through, supporting efforts for a Just Transition away from fossil fuels is a great start, and tackles the issue from a systemic perspective, which is super important. You can find and attend rallies or protests against fossil fuels in your area or organize one yourself. Other ideas are riding a bike for close to home trips instead of driving an automobile and other similar steps to help reduce your own, individual carbon footprint.

• • •

In this chapter, we learned a range of spells designed to combat climate change and its effects, reflecting the solarpunk commitment to ecological activism and sustainable living. These spells, ranging from fostering utopia to protecting homes from climate disasters and promoting renewable energy, are symbolic actions meant to inspire real-world environmental activism. As such, this chapter emphasized the importance of combining magical practices with practical actions, such as volunteering and advocacy, to effect meaningful change in the fight against climate change. Coming up in Chapter Nine, we'll continue creating solarpunk spells to help the environment, but we'll broaden our focus beyond climate change in particular and delve into more general environmental issues.

Chapter Nine: Spells for Other Environmental Issues

limate change is a serious and existential problem that we face as a world community. At the same time, it's not the only environmental concern resulting from capitalism's global dominance. Before most people knew anything about climate change, the environmental movement focused on a variety of other human-caused problems that are still important today. Issues like oil spills, clean air and water, and endangered species, among others. The following chapter, then, focuses on spells to help inspire solarpunk witches to engage in the struggle around these obstacles.

Most of the spells in the previous chapter, with the exception of the two related to renewable energy, are reactionary. Not reactionary in the pejorative political sense, but in the sense that they aren't proactive spells. Rather they're defensive spells used in reaction to some precipitating cause: a storm, a wildfire, a flood, or another extreme climate event that warrants the need for protection. Others react to harmful things about the status quo—like pipelines and coal mining—that help cause those extreme weather events and disasters.

The same is true of this chapter's spells for more general environmental issues. But I want to be sure to start this chapter off with a more proactive, positive, and creation oriented spell. This seed bomb spell is designed to expand the beauty and joy of nature in your community or wherever else you choose to spread the love.

SEED BOMB SPELL

Seed bombs are a wonderful way to spread natural beauty throughout your community regardless of whether you live in a big city, in the suburbs, or out in rural country. They also provide pollen for bees and have other environmental benefits. In addition, seed bombs can be imbued with spells and used as activators to spread love and respect for the Earth.

Supplies:

- A bowl to mix ingredients
- Wildflower seeds or some combination of flowers and wild herbs
- Organic, peat-free compost[105]
- Clay powder[106]
- Water

A note on wildflower seeds before we dive into the spell: you can buy packages that contain a variety of wildflower seeds already mixed together, or you can make your own mix of flower and wild herb seeds. If you'd like, you can also use vegetable seeds from your garden or any other seeds that will do well in your climate zone.[107] Examples of commonly used seeds in seed bombs include chamomile, common spotted orchid, bulbous buttercup, wild thyme, and red clover, among others. Additionally, you should make sure whatever seeds you're using are non-invasive plants that won't disrupt the local ecosystem.

To create your seed bomb spell, use the bowl to mix 5 cups of compost, 2 cups of clay powder, 1 cup of seed blend, and 2 or 3 cups of clay powder

Mix the water in with your hands a little at a time. Be careful not to add too much water too quickly. You aren't making soup.

---

105 Peat is a rapidly depleting resource and is considered to be non-renewable due to the incredibly long time it takes new peat to develop in nature. You can learn more about why it's important to not use peat here: nytimes.com/2022/02/02/realestate/gardening-peat.html.

106 You can find clay powder at most craft stores. If you have a yard with clay-heavy soil, you can use that instead.

107 Knowing which plant-hardiness zone you live in is important for understanding what kinds of plants can grow well in your area, as well as when the best time is to plant them locally. The USDA has a great map for exploring agriculture climate and plant-hardiness zones, and for figuring out which zone you live in: fs.usda.gov/wildflowers/Native_Plant_Materials/Native_Gardening/hardinesszones.shtml

As you use your hands to blend everything together into a paste-like consistency, breathe deeply and feel the energy from your cone of power flowing through you. Feel that power blending and then merging with your intention to spread love for the Earth and nature, as well as your desire to foster a relationship of harmony and balance between your community and the local ecosystem. As your intention merges with the energy you've raised from the Earth and drawn down from the Sun, open yourself up and allow that energy to flow into and fill your seed bomb mixture with the power and magick of your dreams for a better future.

Once you've added all the water, roll the blend into about a dozen small balls that fit comfortably into your throwing hand. Make sure you firmly form and pack the seed bombs so they don't fall apart before you use them. As you roll the seed bombs, continue to focus on your desire and intention.

After all your seed bombs are formed, set them outside to dry in the Sun.

Now you're ready to activate your spells, spread the seeds of your magick and intention, and create natural beauty in your community by throwing the seed bombs into bare patches of Earth. As you throw them, visualize your spell releasing into the physical world.

Spellwork Praxis

This spell is unique from the others in that praxis is, in a very real sense, built into the activation of the spell. By throwing the seed bombs and activating the spell, you're both literally planting flower and herb seeds and metaphorically planting the seeds of your will and intention. Below is an incomplete list of specific and concrete actions you can take to reinforce the magickal spellwork of your seed bombs.

- If you have a yard, plant a garden.

- Plant and leave potted flowers outside around your home for the bees to enjoy[108] and encourage their population recovery.[109]

- If you don't have a yard or space to create a potted garden (or even if you do), research and engage in guerilla gardening.[110]

- Purchase extra seeds to donate to organizations like Seed Savers Exchange and Slow Food USA, or do research to find a local seed library that distributes garden seeds to those who need them.

SPELL FOR OIL SPILL CONTAINMENT

While it's important for us to do positive, creative magic focused on building the utopia world we want for our future, there are also realities we have to contend with now. This is why even though solarpunk is all about hope, it's not a naive hope but a radical one—hope born through struggle against oppression and insurmountable odds. For that reason, it makes sense for a solarpunk witch to be familiar with different types of defense magick, and we've already gone through a variety of defense spells in the previous chapters. Other examples of defense magick include this spell to protect Nature from oil spills and the following spell to protect water from pollution in general.

One of the most immediately visible, damaging effects of the fossil fuel industry, oil spills specifically pose a serious threat to ecological health. When oil spills take place, they pollute water,

---

108 Keep in mind that it's best for the health of your local ecosystems to plant things native to your area. At the very least, do a bit of research to make sure whatever it is you want to plant isn't considered an invasive species in your area.

109 Colony collapse is a serious problem for bee populations. And because of the importance of bees as pollinators, colony collapse is a serious problem for all of us. If you're interested in learning more about colony collapse syndrome, the EPA has an excellent resource on this subject: epa.gov/pollinator-protection/colony-collapse-disorder.

110 Guerrilla gardening is an act of civil disobedience in which gardens are built in neglected urban spaces on public or private land.

beaches, wetlands, and soil; they injure and kill plant and animal life both on land and in water, and they can even cause costly harm to human industries in the area.[111]

The following spell is for use when an oil spill occurs. The spell focuses energy on containment efforts, to help keep the spill and any damage it causes as limited as possible.

Materials:

- A bowl or large cup for mixing your ingredients
- Your athame
- 1.5 cups water
- .5 cups dish soap
- 2 tsp. sugar
- A paperclip

Pour the dish soap into the bowl or large cup. Then, add the water and sugar. Use your athame to stir the ingredients gently until they're well blended, using the athame to channel power into the bubbles as you continue.

As you add your ingredients and stir them together, focus on your intention around containing the oil spill and protecting the animal and plant life in the area. See the water or soil clean and clear. See the animal and plant life in the area alive, clean, healthy, and thriving. Feel the energy of your cone of power flowing through you, and merge that energy with your desire, intention, and willpower. Channel all of that through your athame into your bubble mixture.

After you've created your mixture, make a bubble wand by unfolding the paperclip and bending it into the shape of a tennis racket or pingpong paddle. Alternatively, you can use string or some other kind of non-petroleum based substitute.

111 An analysis by the Tsleil-Waututh Nation Sacred Land Trust found that the overall economic cost of medium to large oil spills runs between $2.4 billion and $9.4 billion: twnsacredtrust.ca/concerns/economic-cost-oil-spill.

When your mixture and wand are ready, it's time to start blowing bubbles and activate your spell. As you breathe and blow bubbles, visualize the oil spill contained to the space within the bubbles, where it can't harm the ecosystem and the life within it. See the oil spill carried away as the bubbles float off into the air and disappear. As you go through that visualization, feel the energy of your cone of power swirling around you and flowing through you. Channel that energy into the containment bubbles you blow so they're charged with both the power of your vision and the power of the Earth and Sun.

Spellwork Praxis

There are a variety of things you can do when oil spills occur. You can volunteer to help with the clean up, send money to organizations aiding the effort, or protest outside gas stations and oil company office buildings. You can also do containment magick to help add to the collective energy being poured into the effort to contain and clean up the oil spill and hold the companies responsible accountable.

SPELL FOR POTION TO HEAL WATER POLLUTION

Clean, fresh water is a necessity for life, not just human life, but all plant and animal life. It's no surprise then that the fight to protect fresh water sources from corporate pollution, and to clean up existing messes, has always been a central part of the environmental movement.

To do spellwork around proactively protecting waterways, you can modify one of the defense magick protection spells we've already gone through here or in the previous chapter, such as the "Spell to Protect Your Home from Climate Disasters" on page 174. Those work great, especially if you're not able to be physically present at the waterway in question. If you are near the waterway, or are able to get to it and be physically present, then you can also use the following potion spell to heal and cleanse the water. This particular spell is written to take place over the course of three days. But it can be modified to be performed in one sitting as well.

Supplies:

- Pestle and mortar to crush and grind herbs

- A cast iron cauldron (or regular cooking pot) for brewing the potion

- A spoon or other stirring utensil (preferably something made of wood or another, but a regular kitchen spoon will work if that's what is available)

- A ceremonial Craft knife, or boline, (or a regular kitchen knife) for cutting up herbs or any other ingredients

- A small or medium sized glass[112] potion bottle

- A glass jar

- Water for the potion base[113]

- Herbs[114]

    - For protection:

        - Garlic (intense cleansing)

        - Blackberry leaf (warding off evil)

        - Black pepper (protection from disease)

    - For healing:

        - Lemon balm (healing)

        - Cinnamon (purification and vitality)

---

112 Avoiding plastic, especially fossil fuel–based plastics, whenever possible is important to solarpunk witches.

113 There are other bases common to potion making, such as alcohol, vinegar, milk, syrups, etc. This spell uses water as a base for two reasons. One, water as a potion base is often associated with cleansing and healing, which is perfect for a spell to protect, cleanse, or heal a waterway. Two, water is better for pouring into a river, lake, or other waterway than something like vinegar, which could potentially harm aquatic life.

114 It's very important to keep in mind that if you're going to pour your potion into a waterway, you need to do research ahead of time to make sure the herbs you use aren't toxic for aquatic life. For example, clove oil can and has been used to euthanize fish.

- Cayenne pepper (clearing bad energy)

Start the spell by filling a large glass jar with about a quarter gallon of water, and then set it out in the Sun to charge. You can use even less water if you want. Just make sure to use enough that, when cooking your potion, it won't all evaporate into steam. You want to make sure there's enough liquid left when finished to have an actual potion rather than just a nice-smelling herbal sludge.

Crack your dried herbs with pestle and mortar. Add the water to your cauldron or pot. Then, add the ingredients and bring the water to a boil. Once the water begins to boil, stir the mixture thoroughly and then remove the cauldron from the heat. Allow the potion to cool, then pour it into a glass jar.

As you go through the instructions above, remember to visualize your intention, blend it with your desire and the cone of power you've raised, and channel that powerful energy into your potion.

Use a lid to cover the top of the jar.Best is a glass lid, or a makeshift lid (with some rubber bands and coffee filters or cheese cloth that can filter out dirt, pollen, etc.), while still allowing sunlight in through the top of the jar. If all you have is a metal lid, that still works fine. Plenty of sunlight will reach the water inside through the sides of the glass jar.

Once you've filled your jar with water and the other spell ingredients, cover it with some kind of lid and set it outside to charge in the Sun's rays for 3 days. If you want or need to perform a shorter spell, you can leave the jar out in the Sun for an hour; there's no reason why your spell shouldn't be just as effective. If you'd like, as you set the jar out in the Sun, say some words such as:

Cleansing, lifegiving solar power,
Charge this water for service to the Earth.
So mote it be.

When you've finished charging your potion, pour it into the polluted waterway. If you don't have access to that waterway, you can pour it into another waterway or your drain to symbolically accomplish the same thing.

Spellwork Praxis

The work around oil spills specifically and water pollution in general are closely related. As such, you can reinforce both spells by doing similar actions. Add power to your spellwork by doing any or all of the following ideas listed below. What other ideas for concrete action can you think of around the issues of clean water and oil spills?

- Organize or participate in river and beach clean up days.

- Pick up litter in parks to help keep soil and natural, open spaces clean.

- Make donations to organizations that rescue and clean animals during oil spills.

- If you're able, volunteer to participate in oil spill clean up efforts.

- Research and boycott companies that invest in or support fossil fuels. Encourage others to boycott those companies as well.

- Organize, participate in, or otherwise support kayaktivist actions[115] and other types of direct actions meant to prevent oil transports, icebreakers, and other fossil fuel support ships from leaving ports.

---

115 Kayaktivism is a type of civil disobedience that uses kayaks and other small boats to disrupt fossil fuel operations. A great example of kayaktivism I participated in took place in May 2015, when activists converged on Seattle using kayaks and water banners to block Shell's Polar Pioneer oil rig from leaving the Port of Seattle: seattletimes.com/seattle-news/environment/paddle-in-seattle-protesters-gather-against-shell-oil-rig/. Only a couple months later in July 2015, a similar protest took place in Portland where we used kayaks and repelled from the St. John's Bridge in an effort to prevent Shell's icebreaker ship, MSV Fennica, from leaving the Port of Portland for the Arctic: opb.org/news/article/shell-icebreaker-portland-protests-delay/.

SPELL TO DISPEL AIR POLLUTION

Like water, clean air is vital. While a living being can likely live in dirty air longer than it can live without potable water, air pollution can still be deadly. Plants can wither, die, or be otherwise negatively affected in poor-quality air. And dirty air for animal life carries serious health effects, including breathing problems and terminal diseases such as cancer.[116]

As with any spell, you can compose and perform this work in numerous ways. You could use candle magick, mental magick, or any of the other myriad forms of magickal spells. For example, you could use fire magick and light a bonfire, cauldron fire, or candles to visualize fire consuming and eliminating air pollution. Or you could draw sigils and other symbols representing air pollution on a piece of parchment and burn the parchment in the fire—more physically, though still symbolically, representing the fire burning away pollution.

To introduce a new type of magick into the mix, the following spell to dispel air pollution uses kinesthetic magick, specifically dance magick. You don't need to know how to dance or even be all that coordinated in order to perform this ritual. So if you aren't a good dancer, don't fret! You can still perform this spell as effectively as a professional dancer could.[117]

Supplies:[118]

---

116 For more information on the negative health impacts of air pollution, the European Environment Agency has a great resource:eea.europa.eu/en/topics/in-depth/air-pollution/eow-it-affects-our-health.

117 Mobility Note: This spell can be performed just as effectively and powerfully if you have limited mobility. For example, if you use a wheelchair or otherwise have difficulty using your legs, you can sit and dance using your torso, arms, and head. Remember, the intention and will and focus behind a spell is more important than the pageantry.

118 Neither of these materials are necessary. You can use your hands instead of a fan, or you can take a piece of paper and fold it into a fan. And you can perform an ecstatic dance without music if you need to or if you prefer. Music can help you keep rhythm and give you sonic peaks and valleys to follow. But it isn't required to perform effective dance magick.

- A hand fan

- A phone or other device to play ecstatic dance music

Use your preferred music app on your device to search "ecstatic dance music." You might want to do this in the day or two prior to your ritual or spellwork to give yourself plenty of time to listen to a variety of examples and choose one you really like, that inspires you and feels in tune with the spell you'll be working.

You don't need to practice or choreograph the dance ahead of time. One of the points of ecstatic dance is to be in the moment, and to move in whatever way that moment compels your body, mind, and spirit.

With your fan in whichever hand feels most comfortable, begin to move to the music in whatever way feels right and comfortable. Move in rhythm with the music, as a counter beat to the music, or a combination of the two. Whatever feels right from moment to moment. If you aren't using music, simply move similarly. You won't have the music to use as a sonic guide for your movements, but perhaps that will be more freeing and allow for a wider variety of movement and kinesthetic form in your spellwork.

As you move, visualize the light of the Sun and the lifeforce of the Earth combined into your cone of power. See it filling you as you move. As you continue to move and as the energy from your cone of power continues to fill your body, your dance becomes more energetic.

You begin moving faster as the energy builds. As your movements and dance build in intensity and the light fills your entire body, that powerful energy explodes out of your hand and into the fan. You begin to wave the fan with rapid back-and-forth movements, and the intensity of your dance continues to build. The energy pouring into your fan is flung up and out as the fan waves through the air.

As that energy travels out from your waving fan, you see that energy consuming and dispelling the poisons and pollution in the air. See the air growing brighter and clearer as it becomes increasingly fresh and clean. Take deep breaths as you continue to move and fan. Notice how sweet the freshening air smells as you physically cleanse the sky. Once you feel the energy peaking, let out a primal scream or guttural shout, belt out a note, or make some other loud and explosive sound with your mouth and vocal chords to release or activate the spell and send it out into the universe.

Don't feel like you have to stop dancing immediately upon releasing the spell. You certainly can stop right away, but it may feel better to continue dancing and wind down the intensity, gradually slowing down and bringing the energy back down with you. This cool-down could also make grounding the final bits of energy easier. But again, as with everything, it's a matter of what works best for you.

Spellwork Praxis

Increase the energy, power, and intention behind your spell by doing the following:

- Research local corporations that emit air pollutants.

- Participate in protests and other direct actions to disrupt big polluters.

- Write letters to people in political office with the power to regulate air quality emissions.

- Use public transportation as much as possible.

- Support efforts to expand and reduce the cost of public transportation service.

- On nice and sunny days, ride a bike instead of using a car or public transportation.

SPELL FOR POTION TO HEAL SOIL

Soil is an invaluable part of ecosystems. From providing habitat for hosts of living creatures in the ecosystem to its role in growing the food we eat, soil and its health can't be overstated.

But due to human activity, healthy soil faces many threats. Its nutrients are depleted. Erosion occurs faster than it should. Corporations irresponsibly and illegally dump toxic waste. Industrial farms—and many smaller farms—soak their crops and soil with herbicides, pesticides, and chemical fertilizers because these harmful methods carry lower costs than more organic methods of food production. But solarpunk is about fostering harmony between humanity and our technology on the one hand, and the Earth and our environment on the other. Things that foster healthy soil, like permaculture practices, are solarpunk as fuck. But poisoning our soil (as well as our water and air) is antithetical to the solarpunk ethos, especially if the main reason for doing so is to increase profit margins for the wealthy at the expense of the public. By working to heal poisoned soil, we cultivate harmony, help move our world toward ecological balance, and ensure we're living our solarpunk values.

Supplies:

- Sun water for the potion's base

- Pestle and mortar to crush and grind herbs

- A cast iron cauldron for brewing the potion (or a regular cooking pot if you don't have a cauldron)

- Spoon or other stirring utensil (Something made of wood or another natural material is preferable. But a regular kitchen spoon will work if that's what is available.)

- A ceremonial Craft knife, or boline, for cutting up herbs or any other ingredients (Again, a regular kitchen knife works perfectly well.)

- A small or medium sized glass potion bottle.

- Herbs

  - Bay leaf (protection and healing)

  - Mint (cleansing)

- Clippings from nitrogen fixing plants such as acacia, white clover, or red clover

Fill a large glass jar with about a quarter gallon of Sun water. You can use less. Just make sure you use enough water that it won't all evaporate into steam when cooking your potion. You need there to be enough liquid left at the end to have a potion instead of just herbal sludge.

Crack your dried herbs with pestle and mortar. Add the water to your cauldron or pot. Then, add the ingredients and bring the water to a boil. Once the water begins to boil, stir the mixture thoroughly and then remove the cauldron from the heat. Allow the potion to cool, then pour it into a glass jar. Use a lid to cover the top of the jar as described in the water pollution healing potion above.

As you're going through the steps above, remember to visualize your intention, blend it with your desire and the cone of power you've raised, and channel that powerful energy into your potion.

Once you've filled your jar with water and covered it with some kind of lid, set it outside to charge in the Sun's rays for three days. If you want or need to perform a shorter spell, you can leave the jar out in the Sun for only a day or for as little as an hour. There's no reason why your spell should be less effective as a result. If you'd like, as you set the jar out in the Sun, say some words such as the following:

Cleansing, lifegiving solar power,
Charge this water for service to the Earth.
So mote it be.

When you've finished charging your potion, pour it into the polluted soil. Of course, be sure to do plenty of research to ensure the herbs you use won't harm or damage the environment and the plant and animal life living in the area.

Spellwork Praxis

Manifest your spell into the physical by taking any or all of the following actions:

- If you have space to do so, compost your yard and food waste to create healthy soil. If you don't have space, do research to find out if there are community composting programs in your area.

- Plant nitrogen fixing plants in your yard and garden, if you have one.

- Clean up trash in parks, forests, and other natural areas to help keep existing soil clean.

- Use public transportation as much as possible to reduce toxic road runoff that can damage soil.

SPELL TO PROTECT SPECIES FROM EXTINCTION

Part of the solarpunk ethos is valuing all life, not just human life. If we're going to create a more balanced and harmonious relationship with nature, then we have to show more respect toward other animal species. We have to shed our perspective of dominion and exploitation over nature. Recognizing the sentience of animals and their right to exist—their right to freedom—is an important first step we can all take within ourselves and encourage within our communities.

Working to save a species on the brink of extinction goes back centuries at least.

In the west, it goes back to the nineteenth century and is directly related to the devastating effects of western imperialism. In the United States and the western territories into which it was violently expanding, Indigenous peoples fought to protect not only their own communities and ways of life, but buffalo and other animal species that were being decimated in the wake of both horse-powered wagon trains and steam-powered locomotives that cut their way through other people's land.

Saving species from extinction took root in Euro-American white culture around the same time through British colonialism in India. In its race to build a navy to dominate the world, the British maritime force was rapidly depleting teak trees, whose hardwood was a staple in shipbuilding back before the days of steel. In order to ensure the Royal Navy had the resources it needed, the British government adopted conservation policies and strategies to help ensure the species of tree didn't disappear.[119]

Here in the U.S., the Endangered Species Act was passed in 1973 and has helped significantly in the fight to save species from extinction at the hands of human activity. However, as we observe extremist right-wing politicians taking power in the U.S, we expect decades of regulatory efforts to be undone in a matter of only a few short years. Now more than ever, it's important to double down in the struggle to save endangered species and, indeed, prevent species from becoming endangered in the first place.

In that spirit then, here is a spell to put energy and intention into the fight to save endangered species from extinction. This spell employs the use of mental magick. As such, you don't need any supplies to perform it. All you need is your desire, intention, visualization, and, if you want, some kind of chant to help build energy and power.

Supplies:

- A quiet space to meditate

- Your imagination

---

119   In a 1662 paper titled, "Sylva," written to the Royal Society, John Evelyn argues the need for forest conservation to ensure the future of the Royal Navy and the British shipbuilding industry. John Evelyn, *Sylva, or A Discourse of Forest-Trees and the Propagation of Timber in His Majesty's Dominions*, with an Essay on the Life and Works of the Author by John Nisbet, Fourth Edition (1706), reprinted London: Doubleday & Co., 1908, V1, p. lxv; online edn, March 2007.

- Your will/desire

Sit in a quiet space and close your eyes. Take deep breaths and visualize your cone of power—the energetic power of the Earth and the light of the Sun—pouring into you, seeping in through your skin, rushing in with each inhale, circling and cycling within you, building up speed and power.

Next, begin to see a representation of the endangered species in your mind's eye. If the endangered species is a penguin, then bring a penguin into your visualization. Or perhaps you'll visualize a gargoyle gecko from New Caledonia. See the animal.

Then, visualize the powerful light energy within you, shooting out of the top of your head and high into the air. Dozens of feet above, the energy reaches a peak and then spills back down, cascading into a sphere of crackling Solar and Earth energy that surrounds the animal you're visualizing. See the energy sphere envelop the animal and its species in a ball of protective power, keeping them safe from harmful impacts of human activity.

In addition to the above spell, other spells already discussed could be helpful here. For example, the spell to reveal the secrets and crimes of corporations and their executives (page 184) could be useful if a particular company's activities are responsible for the destruction of a species habitat. Or if the construction of a road has helped to lead the species' decline, you can visualize the road no longer being used and the species making a resurgence.

With mental magick, you can visualize whatever you desire and infuse the visualization with power and intention. So feel free to be creative in your visualizations and the way you approach this spell to protect endangered species.(Spellwork praxis for this spell will be included in the praxis for the following spell.)

SPELL TO PROTECT RAINFORESTS AND OLD GROWTH FORESTS

Trees are often called the lungs of the Earth.[120] They play a vital role in natural carbon sequestration.[121] Like all plants, trees use photosynthesis to convert sunlight, water, and . . . the infamous greenhouse gas, carbon dioxide, into energy. This means that the more trees we lose to deforestation, the harder it becomes to fight climate change. We lose a vital ally in the struggle.

Old growth forests, which are even more adept at carbon extraction than younger forests,[122] are often targeted for timber. Large rainforests, such as the Amazon in particular, are targeted for deforestation in order to clear land for farms and cattle ranches.[123]

There are a variety of angles from which you can approach spellwork to protect the rainforest. You can use defense spells like the mental magick above by visualizing a massive wall or sphere protecting the forest. Another option is to come at it from more of a growth and regenerative perspective. For this, a plant magick spell like the following is a great choice.

Supplies:

- A sapling or seed[124]

---

120 It's important to note that the oceans and, for example, kelp forests, are arguably at least as important as trees on land in terms of being the lungs of the Earth. For more information, check out this resource from SGK Planet: sgkplanet.com/en/are-the-oceans-lungs-of-the-earth.

121 According to Frank Mitloener, a UC Davis professor who works in this field, "Carbon sequestration is the process of capturing, securing and storing carbon dioxide from the atmosphere. The idea is to stabilize carbon in solid and dissolved forms so that it doesn't cause the atmosphere to warm":clear.ucdavis.edu/explainers/what-carbon-sequestration.

122 The following source has more information on how size and age affects trees importance in the fight against climate change: news.mongabay.com/2019/05/tall-and-old-or-dense-and-young-which-kind-of-forest-is-better-for-the-climate.

123 For more on how cattle ranching drives Amazon deforestation, see this Climate Policy Initiative resource on this subject: climatepolicyinitiative.org/publication/the-economics-of-cattle-ranching-in-the-amazon-land-grabbing-or-pushing-the-agricultural-frontier.

124 Again, it is always a best practice to use plants that are local and non-invasive to the area in which you live. This is especially true if you'll be planting directly into the

- Organic planting soil

- Sun water

- Organic nutrients

- A planting pot

If you have a spot where you can plant the sapling or seed directly into the ground, you can certainly do so. But if you are using a seed, it's easier to successfully sprout and grow a seed in a pot. Even if you use a sapling, you may want to plant and transplant it into pots until it's grown and gained some strength. It's entirely up to you though.

The sapling can be a tree, but it doesn't have to be. What's important is that it's a plant that you can tend to and care for. It's a physical representation of the forest that you can watch grow into a strong, thriving, and healthy life.

If you use a pot, you can also gather materials such as markers, paint and brushes, glitter, or anything else you want to use to decorate the pot with symbolic colors, magickal symbols, and other art. Again, this is entirely optional, depending on your preferences. If you aren't much for art and decorating, that's perfectly fine and you can still create and perform a spell that's no less effective.

As you plant the seed or sapling, as you decorate the pot, visualize the future you desire. See the old growth or rainforest (of course, it's entirely possible the forest you're thinking of is both) as a strong, thick, vibrant, healthy, thriving ecosystem. Blend this vision with the Sun and Earth energy you combined into your cone of power. Then infuse the seeds or sapling, the pot, and any art or symbols you created—infuse it all with your powerful vision of a better future with safe and healthy forests.

Over the months or years, depending on the kind of plant you choose, care for your spell. Water the plant and if needed feed it

ground but is also a good practice to keep in mind even if your plant will only ever be in a pot.

organic nutrients. Transplant it into larger pots as necessary to allow it room to grow and thrive. If possible, find a place to plant it directly in the Earth (planting in the ground is not necessary for an effective spell).

Each time you carry out these caretaker tasks, do the healthy forest visualization and recharge the spell. You can even see your role as caretaker for this one plant as representative of humanity's relationship with the forest and with nature in general. As such, you could also include visualization of humanity's relationship with nature growing stronger and more harmonious as the plant grows and becomes stronger itself.

Spellwork Praxis
Saving endangered species and forest protection are closely related in many ways. The material actions you can take to help manifest your spellwork in the physical world for both issues is also similar. Reinforce the magick of both kinds of spells by doing any or all of the following:

- Research and refrain from purchasing products made from wood and other resources that come from the Amazon, or other areas of mass habitat destruction.

- Donate to on-the-ground organizations and organizations that use radical tactics in the fight to protect endangered animals, their habitat, and old growth forest.

- Engage in or otherwise support active tree sits.

- Support efforts to end factory farming and other corporate animal abuse practices.

- If you need to buy wood products, whenever possible, buy products made with reused and recycled wood.

- If you eat meat, cut back on how much you consume or even consider becoming a vegetarian.

•   •   •

In this chapter, we expanded on the spellwork we learned in Chapter Eight, focusing on broader issues beyond climate change, such as oil spills, water and air pollution, and soil degradation. Chapter Nine introduced both proactive and reactive spells to inspire solarpunk witches to engage in environmental activism. As always, we encouraged a hands-on approach to environmental stewardship, blending spellwork with practical efforts to build a sustainable future.

Chapter Ten: Spells to Fight Fascism, Capitalism, and Other Global Problems

Solarpunk isn't just about solutions to climate change. Building utopia requires more than environmentalism. It requires social justice. In fact, without a solid social and racial justice analysis,125 our environmentalism—even where successful in and of itself—takes us only a small part of the way toward a better, utopian world.

With that in mind, the following chapter includes spells for the struggle around social justice issues other than environmental concerns. Important, and very solarpunk, things like stopping the current rise of neo-fascism throughout the world, ending capitalism and adopting more compassionate and cooperative economic systems, ending white supremacy and patriarchy, fostering safe communities for queer and trans folks, creating peace and ending war, and more.

LAND ACKNOWLEDGMENT AND RESTORATION SPELL

A land acknowledgment and restoration spell is a great way to honor the land you live on and its Indigenous inhabitants. This spell serves a variety of important purposes for a non-Indigenous solarpunk witch. One, it's a means of acknowledging that you're living on stolen land. It's a way of respecting that land and the people who have lived on it for millennia before we moved in. It also acknowledges the harm colonialism has done, both to those the land was taken from and to the land itself. Finally, it's the most respectful

---

125 In this context, a solid social and racial justice analysis should account for environmental racism and the role of imperialism in environmental degradation, both historically and in modern times. It should also touch on concepts like Just Transition and the importance of following the lead of those most affected by climate change and other injustices.

and non-appropriative way I'm aware of by which you can get to know the energies and spirits of the land you live on, especially if you're a settler colonizer.

Before you begin, take some time to research the peoples who are Indigenous to the area you live in. For me, that means learning about the Kalapuya people, both their history and their present, both practical facts about them (such as their traditional foods and building materials) as well as their spiritual practices and the ways in which they have woven those practices into their daily lives. Understand that this spell is not a replacement for direct action and support of Indigenous communities, which will be discussed below in the spellwork praxis section.

Materials:

- A map of your local county (a simple, hand-drawn map is fine)

- A small bowl of local soil

- A responsibly sourced green or brown candle made from soy or beeswax

- Cedar-elderberry incense (use what makes the most sense for the area in which you live)

- Lavender and blackberries

Begin by preparing your sacred space in the way you usually do. For this ritual, I decorate my altar with lavender and blackberry flowers or branches because those are common plants here where I live. Depending on where you live, you might want to use different plants for your altar decorations during this spell. Next, light your incense and smudge your surroundings and yourself, inviting in positive energy and clarity.

Place the map in front of you. Place your hands over it, close your eyes, and ground yourself, feeling your connection with the land beneath you.

Light the candle, saying,

*I light this flame in honor of the traditional
inhabitants and custodians of this land.
May their spirit and resilience continue to burn bright
far into the future.*

Take the bowl of soil in your hands, feeling its texture and temperature. Connect with it as a representation of the Earth and the land that has been cared for by these people for thousands of years.

Speak aloud your acknowledgment, something like:

*I acknowledge that I inhabit the land of Indigenous peoples
[name specific groups if possible].
Their care and wisdom have shaped these lands for thousands of
years.
I recognize the harm that colonization has inflicted upon them
and their lands. In the spirit of reparation and restoration,
I commit to respecting, listening to, and supporting
Indigenous peoples and their sovereignty.*

Now, focus on the soil in your hands and say,

*May the Earth heal.
May the Indigenous peoples of this land [name specific groups if
possible] prosper again.
May justice be served and balance restored.*

Return the soil back to the Earth, ideally outdoors in a spot where it won't be disturbed. As you do so, envision the positive energies from your spell sinking into the ground, infusing the land with the intent of restoration and respect.

Close the spell by saying,

*I make this acknowledgment and
commitment not only in words,
but also in action.
In the name of justice, restoration, and respect,
so mote it be.*

Let the candle burn down safely, its light a symbol of ongoing commitment to honor the land and its Indigenous custodians.

Again, remember, a land acknowledgment and restoration spell is not a one-time action, but a commitment to continual learning, respect, and tangible support for Indigenous communities. Use this spell as a reminder and focal point for your actions in support of Indigenous sovereignty, land back initiatives, and social justice efforts.

Spellwork Praxis

After performing a land acknowledgment and restoration spell, one of the most practical and meaningful actions a solarpunk witch can undertake is to engage directly with local Indigenous communities and the environment. Here are a few suggestions:

1. Support Indigenous Organizations: Research local Indigenous organizations that are working on issues like land rights, cultural preservation, education, and social justice. Make a donation, volunteer your time, or use your platform to raise awareness about their work.

2. Attend Indigenous-led Events: Look for public events in your community, such as talks, workshops, or cultural festivals led by Indigenous people. Attending these events not only supports Indigenous communities but also provides an opportunity for learning and understanding.

3. Environmental Restoration: Participate in local environmental restoration projects. This can involve planting native species, cleaning up litter, removing

invasive species, or participating in citizen science projects to monitor local wildlife. These actions align with the spirit of the spell, contributing to the healing and restoration of the land.

4. Advocate for Land Back Initiatives: Learn about land back initiatives in your area. These might involve returning public land to Indigenous control or supporting Indigenous sovereignty. Get involved by attending public meetings, writing to your elected officials, or campaigning in your community.

5. Education: Commit to continual learning about the history, culture, and contemporary issues facing the Kalapuya people and other Indigenous communities. Share this knowledge with others in your community to foster greater understanding and respect.

Remember, the goal is to ensure that your actions align with the intentions of your spellwork and are respectful, supportive, and beneficial to the Indigenous communities you are seeking to acknowledge and honor.

SPELL TO BRING CHAOS TO FASCIST ORGANIZATIONS

For decades, socialists, anarchists, and others on the far left have warned of an impending resurgence of fascist organization and activity. The rise of neo-fascism throughout the world started becoming more apparent with the seemingly sudden and rapid growth of the Alt-Right movement.[126] In reality, that movement had been festering in the dark recesses of the internet for years. In that time, we on the left have generally been called hyperbolic by both centrist liberals and conservatives.

---

126 The Southern Poverty Law Center has a great resource for more information on the Alt-Right and its threat to marginalized communities: splcenter.org/fighting-hate/extremist-files/ideology/alt-right.

It was only with the publicly racist rhetoric and policy ideas of Donald Trump during his first presidential campaign back in 2015 and 2016—and particularly his electoral college victory that unjustly lifted him to the presidency—that the fascist white supremacists lurking in the basements of society felt bold enough to emerge from the back corners of the internet. They became a physical presence and a very real and dangerous threat in the world.[127] It was also then that, finally, a larger portion of U.S. society started taking the threat of fascism seriously.

Still, even today, going on a decade later—after an attempted fascist coup to prevent Trump from leaving office, after white supremacist and ultra nationalists gangs have been brawling in the streets,[128] and as the extremist Christofascist right wing ramps up a renewed campaign of legal and physical violence against drag queens, trans folks, and other queer people across the country[129]— there are plenty on both the right and left who don't take this issue seriously, or at least not seriously enough. There are those who continue to insist that we just need to vote harder, despite the infrequency with which the popular vote reflects who sits in the Oval Office, and even though conservatives have gerrymandered voting districts to the point that voting for many is literally useless. There are even those who openly or silently support the fascist

---

127 PBS has an excellent documentary called *Documenting Hate: Charlottesville*, which dives into the 2017 Unite the Right rally, which amounted to a violent coming-out riot for the alt-right and included overtly racist, anti-Semitic, and homophobic marches, chants, and displays, combined with gang violence, intimidation, and the murder of counter protester Heather Heyer: pbs.org/wgbh/frontline/documentary/ documenting-hate-charlottesville.

128 For example, there was a street brawl in Oregon City, Oregon on June 24, 2023 between the Proud Boys (cis-hetero supremacists and self-described "western chauvinists") and Rose City Nationalists (a white supremacist, neo-nazi organization). More details can be found in coverage from *Oregon Live* and the *Daily Mail*: oregonlive. com/crime/2023/06/2-arrested-during-brawl-between-proud-boys-nationalists-protesting-oregon-city-pride-police-and-witness-say.html and dailymail.co.uk/news/ article-12234365/Proud-Boys-group-unmask-neo-Nazis-beat-American-flag-pole-Pride-parade-Oregon.html.

129 This is a good starting place for more information on the recent right wing attacks on trans folks. cnn.com/2023/04/30/politics/republicans-transgender-attacks-statehouse-haley-trump/index.html

gangs now roaming our streets and the fascist ideas and precepts seeping into mainstream political discourse.

Fascists certainly have their own twisted and vile notions about what a utopian society looks like. Of course, solarpunk witches categorically and emphatically reject those ideas, and the very existence of such fascist visions of utopia is why our solarpunk dreams about and work toward building utopia needs to include solid antifascist and antiracist political education.

The following spell uses sigil magick to cause chaos in fascist organizations.

Supplies:

- Parchment paper
- Pen or pencil
- A lighter, matches, or Sun water (to activate your sigil)

First, write out your spell with words. Keep it short, simple, and to the point. I often use all capital letters. But feel free to use lower case if you prefer. A couple examples include:

- DESTROY FASCISTS[130]
- CHAOS AMONG FASCISTS
- CONFUSION WITHIN FASCIST ORGANIZING
- DISTRUST AMONG FASCISTS

Next, use those letters and their forms to create a sigil. You don't have to use every piece of every letter, though you certainly can. Use the pieces you want. If you're inspired to add something that isn't included in your letter shapes, that's okay too. What is important is that the sigil is meaningful and powerful for you.

Using the first first phrase, DESTROY FASCISTS, I came up with the following sigil:

---

130 It should be reiterated here that this book doesn't advocate endangering or physically harming anyone. You don't have to physically attack fascists in order to destroy their influence and ability to harm others.

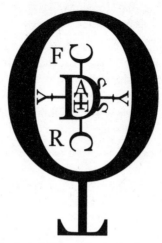

"Destroy fascists" sigil (illustration by Justine Norton-Kertson)

Of course, while you're creating your sigil, you'll want to be in a quiet and solitary place if possible (unless you're creating a group sigil for group magick). Focus on your intention, visualize your phrase as reality in whatever way makes most sense to you, and infuse your sigil with the magick of your visualization combined with your cone of power. You don't have to activate your sigil right away if you don't want to. But if you wait, when you're ready to activate it, be sure to repeat the visualization and recharge the sigil.

When you feel the energy you are infusing into your sigil is at a peak, do something to activate the sigil. Burning the paper the sigil is written on is probably the most common method, as mentioned earlier in the book. You can also put it in water until it dissolves. I've known people to tear up a sigil and release the shreds into the wind. However, I don't recommend this method because littering isn't good for our communities. (Spellwork praxis for this spell will be included in the praxis for the following spell.)

SPELL TO BIND SUPREMACISTS

White supremacy, patriarchy, cis-straight supremacy, and other types of supremacist attitudes are outgrowths of and rooted in fascist ideology. At the heart of fascism is the belief in essential identities. For fascists, what they insist are essential, natural, and unchangeable identities exist in a strict and similarly essential hierarchy. They believe it's their natural right to rule over those who are lower on the ladder, and they believe it's their right to use the violent force and power of the state in order to enforce their perceived hierarchy.

Because of the fact that supremacism and fascism are so closely related, these global afflictions can be approached, magickally speaking, from similar angles. You could easily adapt the above sigil magick to apply to white supremacist organizations or patriarchy. And like with most magickal work, you could find and create a way to perform a spell using just about any magickal methodology.

One good option in this particular case is doing a binding spell to help ensure supremacists can't do harm to you and others. Binding spells are a great way of using magick to keep people from harming others, and, for many witches, are a generally preferred alternative to spellwork aimed at attacking and physically harming people. You can refer back to the "Magickal Ethics" section in the Introduction section (on page 11) for a refresher on the idea of doing this kind of magickal work without the intention of causing physical harm to others.

Supplies:

- Cordage, ribbon, or string
- An image or other physical symbol that for you represents racists, gender essentialists, or other supremacists

Wrap the physical symbol with the cord, string, ribbon, or something similar.[131] As you do so, envision these groups immobilized,

---

131 For example, if you're binding homophobes, you may or may not want to use rainbow ribbon instead of regular cord, rope, or string.

impotent, incapable of doing physical, emotional, psychological, or spiritual harm to others. As you wrap the symbol and visualizing the binding, say the following:

Powers of Earth, Air, Fire, and Water,
Universe and mighty ancestors
I call upon you to bind
(white, gender, religious . . .) supremacists
so they can do no harm to any living being.

Bind them from
infringing upon our freedom of self-expression
and right to happiness.
Bind them from spreading hatred and fear.
Bind them from using
systems and laws to marginalize other communities.
And bind all who
enable supremacists in their vile work.

In the name of justice,
of compassion and equality,
I bind them,
their lips and tongues.
I bind their deeds.
No harm may they bring.
So mote it be!

Spellwork Praxis

Fascists, and more generally, supremacists, have similar worldviews and values. Therefore, the work of bringing chaos to fascist organizations and the work of binding supremacists are intertwined. Below is a list of material work you can do to manifest your magickal work from the two spells above.

- Research, find, and support your local Antifa network. If you can't find one in your area, consider starting your own.[132]

- Join a local Black Lives Matter chapter or other organization actively engaged in antiracist work.[133]

- Engage in self-reflection to recognize your own privilege and the way systems of power uphold that privilege.

- Attend or organize community defense and other antifascist action training.[134]

- Research ways to support and engage in radical queer organizing and community defense efforts.[135]

SPELL TO SEED SAFE COMMUNITIES

Utopia without safe communities is a gross contradiction. So how do we create safe communities? One key factor is to change the way in which we "police" our society. Modern police organizations employ full-time public relations teams tasked with creating an illusion of cops as heroes and public servants who are here to protect, but the truth is much less noble. While it's well beyond the scope of this

---

132 The Anarchist Library has a great resource on how to form your own Antifa group: theanarchistlibrary.org/library/forming-an-antifa-group.

133 Arizona State University has a list of national racial justice organizations that provides a decent starting point for anyone who wants to start actively engaging in antiracist work: libguides.law.asu.edu/c.php?g=1047490&p=7601586.

134 Power Shift Network has lots of great manuals and resources related to community defense organizing: powershift.org/resources/community-defense-zone-starter-guide.

135 Movement Advancement Project has a comprehensive list of resources and organizations for those who want to start engaging in work around LGBTQIA+ issues: lgbtmap.org/resource-page.

book to get into the history and sociological function of modern police departments, it can briefly be summarized with the following basic facts:

- Modern police departments are descendants of violent and inhumane slave hunters and catchers.[136]
- Modern police forces have, since their inception, been the frontline soldiers in the capitalist war against the working class, being used to infiltrate unions as well as violently attack, arrest, and kill workers to break strikes.[137]
- Police forces, as part of their official duty and capacity, enforced the system and institutions of racial segregation, and waged a violent war against civil rights protesters.[138]
- Cops made up a significant portion of the Ku Klux Klan back in its heyday, engaging in vigilante justice against people of color in southern communities.[139]

---

136 *Our Enemies in Blue: Police and Power in America* by Kristian Williams is a great book on this topic that isn't overly academic and therefore is a relatively easy read: akpress.org/our-enemies-in-blue.html. And while this idea that modern policing descended from slave catchers may seem controversial to many, it isn't. In fact, even police organizations themselves admit to this legacy. See, for example, this article from the National Law Enforcement Officers Memorial Fund: nleomf.org/slave-patrols-an-early-form-of-american-policing.

137 A great book on the role police play in protecting business interests rather than public interest is *Policing a Class Society: The Experience of American Cities, 1865-1915* by Sidney L. Harring.

138 The city of Detroit in the late 1950s and early 1960s is a great case study on the role police and police brutality played in racial segregation during the civil rights era. For more, see this resource from the University of Michigan History Labs:policing. umhistorylabs.lsa.umich.edu/s/detroitunderfire/page/1958-63.

If you're interested in how police continue this legacy today of enforcing a social order rooted in racial exclusion and control, Tufts University has a great article titled, "How Racial Segregation and Policing Intersect in America": now.tufts.edu/2020/06/17/how-racial-segregation-and-policing-intersect-america.

139 *LEO Weekly* published a great article about Louisville, Kentucky's historical relationship between the KKK and police:, leoweekly.com/news/louisvilles-forgotten-history-of-police-officers-in-the-kkk-15761518.

Unfortunately, like many problems with policing and institutionalized police departments, white supremacy and KKK membership among police officers continues to be an issue today, as detailed in this article from the *Lewis & Clark Law Review*: law. lclark.edu/live/files/28080-lcb231article2johnsonpdf.

- Police are at the forefront of the so-called War on Drugs, which has led to the mass incarceration and default, constitutionally protected re-enslavement of people of color.[140]
- The ranks of KKK-descendent organizations like the Oath Keepers, III%, and Proud Boys are known to be full of cops.[141]

The above list is incomplete, but sufficient, to make two main points: 1) that the primary role of police is and has always been to protect and defend institutional wealth and power, and 2) the primary means of accomplishing that has been the violent over-policing and incarceration of U.S. people of color in particular, and poor working people in general.

For this spell, we'll use plant magic similar to the spell we reviewed in Chapter Five's section on Ostara, or the Spring Equinox, celebration.

Supplies:
- A planting pot
- Soil
- Flower seeds
- Sun water
- Decorating supplies:
    - Markers
    - Paints

---

140 *The New Jim Crow: Mass Incarceration in the Age of Colorblindness* by Michelle Alexander, a civil rights lawyer, legal scholar, and one of the founders of the Black Lives Matter organization, details mass incarceration's effects on Black America, and the role police play in the Drug War and other tools of mass incarceration. The book's website also has a wealth of resources, including a study guide for the book and organizing guides. newjimcrow.com.
141 In 2020, the Brennan Center for Justice published *Hidden in Plain Sight: Racism, White Supremacy, and Far-Right Militancy in Law Enforcement*, an excellent study detailing the historical and current problem of police participation in and sympathy with white supremacists organizations: brennancenter.org/our-work/research-reports/hidden-plain-sight-racism-white-supremacy-and-far-right-militancy-law.

- Glitter
- Glue
- Boline
- Wall pin or string
- A cauldron or firepit
- Materials for a fire (candles, wood…)
- Matches or a lighter

Fill the pot with soil. Use your finger to poke holes in the dirt up to your first knuckle. Drop seeds in the holes and cover them. Feed with Sun water.

As you plant the seeds, focus on your intention for safe communities. See police cars abandoned and rusted out. Visualize police stations being converted into community centers. See prisons being gutted, redesigned on the interior, and turned into free housing for the houseless. See people of all backgrounds coming together in your community and interacting in peace, trust, harmony. See this intention fusing with your cone of power and flowing into seed and soil. Care for your seed. Feed it. Give it magickal sunlight. Watch it sprout, grow, and bloom into a beautiful flower.

When your flower has bloomed, use your boline to cut the stem near the soil. As you do, say the following words, or something similar:

Like the seed that sprouts and blooms
into a beautiful and fragrant flower,
so too does our community grow stronger
in harmony and peace.
So mote it be.

Take your freshly-cut flower and pin it to your wall to dry. Alternatively, if you don't want to put pin holes in your wall, you can tie a length of string to the end of the flower's stem, then tie the other end of the string to something already available that allows the flower to hang upside down to dry. Once you've hung your flower to dry, repeat the following or similar words:

The stillness and beauty of this flower is
preserved for generations to come,
a symbol of the safety engendered by the
sustaining power of peaceful cooperation
in our community.
So mote it be.

After the flower is dry, set it out in the Sun to charge for twenty-four hours. Then, light a sacred fire in your cauldron and burn the flower to release your spell into the Universe.

Spellwork Praxis

Like the other spells in this book, there are a number of actions you can and should take in the physical world to reinforce your magick and manifest your spell. Such actions include but aren't limited to:

- Researching and finding a way to materially support organizations working to end police brutality
- Attending workshops on mediation
- Learning about and practicing restorative justice
- Vocally and actively supporting, and attending, protests against police brutality
- Attending a city council meeting and speaking in support of cutting police funding

SPELL TO END CAPITALISM AND WESTERN IMPERIALISM

Capitalism is the system of economic exploitation at the root of so many of our world's social problems. Different but closely related is western imperialism, which, at its most basic, is capitalism's violent spread around the world: its attempt to bring all labor and so-called markets under its power and control. Plainly stated, capitalism is a system where the people who own the means of economic production like land, factories, etc.—the owner-bosses—exploit the labor of others to make money for themselves.

From institutionalized white supremacy to systemic poverty and police brutality, from oil spills and climate change to resource wars and disaster profiteers, capitalism and capitalists encourage and utilize the worst in humanity as tools to maintain wealth and power. If we want to resolve these big problems in a way that amounts to more than a bandaid, then we need to end capitalism and replace it with an economic system rooted in compassion and cooperation rather than greed and competition.

Just ending capitalism isn't enough without ensuring the system it's replaced with isn't just as bad or even worse. What's the use in eliminating capitalism if it means a return to slavery? Or if it means fascism rises to global power? For that reason, the following spell focuses on the future economy we want to build, rather than focusing on capitalism and its demise.

One great way to do this is with plant magick, like with the spell above. Plant magick is longer-term than a lot of spells and so fits well with the monumental task of upsetting the global socio-economic and political order.

Another option is to do art magick. The following spell is a great example of art magick put to the purpose of fighting capitalism and imperialism.

Materials needed:
- A large canvas or piece of paper
- Art supplies (paints, markers, crayons, collage materials, etc.)
- A small dish of salt
- Incense (such as sage or sandalwood)
- A candle (preferably green or white)
- A feather

Begin by casting a magickal circle to protect your space during your working. Then, cleanse your tools by lighting incense and letting the smoke waft over your art materials and your canvas to cleanse them. As you do so, say, "By Air and Fire, I cleanse these tools."

Next, charge your materials by taking a small bowl of salt water and sprinkling a little on your art materials and canvas, saying, "By Earth and Water, I bless thee."

The next step is to set your intention. Light your candle and sit before your canvas. As you gaze into the flame, visualize a world without capitalism and imperialism. Imagine what that world might look like, feel like, sound like. Hold that vision in your mind and heart; let it fill you with determination and hope.

Once you've combined your intention and the power of your will, it's time to create your art. Begin to translate your vision onto your canvas. Don't worry about it being a perfect piece of art. Don't worry if it looks "good" or if anyone would look at it and say, "Wow, that's some awesome art!" The important thing is that it's meaningful to *you*. As you create, keep your intention in mind. Let your feelings about capitalism and imperialism flow into the artwork. You might want to chant something like,

Change takes root,
power is shared,
systems shift,
bonds are repaired.

Once your artwork is complete, take the feather and wave it over the canvas, imagining your intention being sealed into the artwork. As you do this, say,

By the power of Air,
I send my will into the universe.
As I will it,
so mote it be.

Spellwork Praxis

The spell is complete, but don't just put your art away. Hang it in a place where you'll see it often. Use it as a focal point for meditation. Show it to others, if you feel comfortable doing so, and use it to start conversations about capitalism and imperialism.

There's no shortage of other specific and material things you can do to help reinforce your anti-capitalist spellwork. Examples include, but aren't limited to the following

- Join a labor union or organize one in your workplace.

  - Support other union workers and workers who are fighting for a union.

  - Never cross a picket line.

- Support or otherwise engage in sit-ins and shutdowns of anti-worker, anti-environment businesses.

- Attend or organize protests against union busting companies.

- Join a socialist organization or anarchist affinity group.

- Research and learn about alternative economic systems based on cooperation, human need, and environmental stewardship.

- Start or join a mutual aid group.

NO MORE BORDERS SPELL

Borders are one of the tools capitalists use to control the movement and labor of the working class. They're artificial lines rooted in western imperialism. The world's national borders are based on the lines drawn when European imperialists, including those who colonized the Americas, carved up the globe in their race to dominate and control global populations, labor, and markets.

Ending borders would upturn systems of power all over the planet. And while any broad system change will have far-reaching effects, ending borders wouldn't be any more disruptive than capitalism, or than white supremacy and climate change. Regardless of the fact that ending borders would be disruptive, ultimately, it would create more freedom of movement, help reunite immigrant and refugee families all over the world, and enable a more stable, balanced socio-economic system.[142] In short, it could be a powerful tool for justice and in ending capitalist exploitation and domination.

A great way to do spellwork to end borders is with some cord and knot magick, as outlined in the spell below.

Supplies:

- A 1 ft. length of cord or something similar like string or ribbon

- A boline or pair of scissors

Get a cord that's about a foot long. The cord represents borders. Recognizing that a goal such as ending borders could likely be long-term work, tie four knots in the cord, roughly one per quarter foot. The knots represent complications in the operation and function of borders that will help lead to their dissolution. As you tie the knots, visualize those complications. One option is to visualize a mass exodus of border patrol agents that results in border checkpoint closures across the U.S. Southwest.

After you've tied the knots—complications—into the chord, focus your intention for a world free from borders. Merge that focus with the cone of power you raised during your ritual. Allow that energy to flow through you and into your boline or scissors. Visualize them being charged by the power of your intention. Then—

Cut the cord.

Sever the borders.

---

142 In fact, many economists argue that open borders would be a massive boon for the global economy, potentially doubling global GDP. See this WBUR (NPR) article for more information: wbur.org/hereandnow/2018/08/06/open-borders-economy-workers.

Repeat this spell as often as you want, or as often as you need to keep you inspired and invigorated in the fight for immigrant and refugee justice.

Spellwork Praxis

Once you've completed your spell to end borders, it's time to get to the work of manifesting your magick in the physical world. Examples of ways you can do that include, but aren't limited to the following:

- Find and support organizations run by and for immigrants.
- Join your local antifascist network or other group fighting against borders and for the rights of immigrants and refugees.
- Find and take community defense training.
- Do research and find out if there is an ICE raid hotline in your area. If so, share it on your social media pages to help spread the word about it.
- Go meet people from immigrant and refugee communities in your region.
  - Make an effort to learn about their cultures.
  - Show them that they're welcome and have broader community support.

•   •   •

Solarpunk recognizes the intersectional nature of climate change and other environmental health issues. It's with that in mind that our focus in this chapter has been global challenges such as fascism, capitalism, queerphobia, and white supremacy. WE dove into detailed spellwork for acknowledging and restoring Indigenous lands, disrupting fascist organizations, and fostering safe, inclusive communities. And like the other chapters in this section, we took the time to encourage complementing our spiritual practices with active participation in socio-political movements for a more equitable world.

Chapter Eleven: Creating Your Own Spells

*T*here's absolutely nothing wrong with using preexisting spells, either in whole or in part. At the same time, there's something incredibly personal and satisfying about creating and working your *own* spell. Creating your own spells is an empowering way to tailor your magickal practice to your unique needs, situations, goals, and spiritual journey. It also aligns with the solarpunk ethos and dedication to the Do It Yourself movement. With that in mind, then, what follows is an easy to use, step-by-step guide to help you craft your own solarpunk witchcraft spells.

1. Define Your Intention

   Begin by clarifying your intention—what it is you want the spell to accomplish, your desired final outcome? It should be specific, positive, and framed in the present tense. For example, instead of saying, "I want to stop climate change," say, "I am actively participating in creating a sustainable world" or "I am taking action, and I am part of the solution to climate change." This helps you to direct your energies towards your goal in a constructive way.

2. Choose Your Magickal Elements

   Depending on your intention, you might want to draw on the energy of the sun, the Earth, or both. You may even want to draw in elements associated with other planets, depending on the work you're doing. Do you want to use herbs, stones, or essential oils? What about symbols, sigils, or representations of archetypes? What about elements of art, culinary, or kinesthetic magick? Decide on what elements will best serve your intention.

3. Select a Time and Place

The timing of your spell can enhance its effectiveness. Consider various magickal correspondences such as lunar phases, solar events, or even specific days of the week and times of day. Likewise, choose a location that resonates with your intention. It could be your altar, outdoors, or a particular room in your house.

4. Compose Your Words

What words, incantations, or affirmations will you use to convey your intention, if any? Remember to keep them positive and present tense. Writing them down can help you focus your thoughts.

5. Plan Your Actions

Think about what actions you'll perform during the spell. This could be anything from lighting a candle to drawing a sigil, from mixing herbs to a series of movements or dances. Use your knowledge of magickal correspondences to plan out how each of these actions symbolize your intention.

6. Perform Your Spell

Using the example of the basic ritual for solarpunk witches outlined in Chapter Four, or in whatever other way you prefer, cast your circle, call your quarters, invoke deities/archetypes if you choose to do so, and do whatever other ritual components you might design as part of your spell. Then perform your spell as you've planned it. Speak your words, do your actions, and hold your visualization as strongly as possible.

7. Ground Your Energy

After performing the spell, ground your energy. This could involve eating something, meditating, or simply spending time in nature. Many people place their palms on the ground to let excess energy drain from their bodies back into the Earth. It helps to balance your energy and allows you to integrate the magick you've done.

8. Close Your Circle

Close your circle in whatever way you prefer. This could include the ceremony of using an athame to unwind and erase the circle, as well as a besom to sweep away the boundary. Or it could be as simple as saying a few words of thanks to any energies, deities, archetypes, elements, or other spirits you've called upon.

9. Follow through with Practical Actions

Finally, reinforce the energy of your spell by taking practical actions in the physical world. If your spell was about protecting the environment, for example, you might follow through by volunteering for a local conservation project.

Remember, there are no set rules in witchcraft, only guidelines. Your practice is your own, so feel free to adapt these steps in any way that best suits you and your personal practice. Always remember that what's most important is that your spells are meaningful to you, and that they align with your solarpunk vision for a better and more just future.

Happy spellcrafting!

Conclusion: Embracing the Sun, Embracing the Future

As we draw this book to a close, it's my hope that you've found within its pages not only a set of tools, rituals, correspondences, and spells, but also a new perspective by which to view and interact with the world around you—a new framework for your Craft spirituality and practice. Solarpunk witchcraft, in essence, is a vision of a future where we align ourselves with the natural rhythms of the Earth and the Sun, while harnessing the best of our human ingenuity and creativity. Through the merging of radical politics, optimism, sustainability, and the transformative power of magick, we find a path forward that honors both our planet and its inhabitants.

This book has invited you to consider the principles of solarpunk as a viable and necessary blueprint for a future marked by both ecological consciousness and social justice. It has asked you to examine the power dynamics of our world, to recognize the oppressive structures of capitalism, imperialism, cishet-white supremacy, and the like, and to envision a future where such systems no longer have a stranglehold on our planet or our lives.

Together, we've explored the deeply interwoven relationship between witchcraft and solarpunk, finding common ground in their shared reverence for nature, resilience, and the inherent power within us all to enact change, both in our lives and in the larger world around us. We"ve delved into the potent magick of the Sun and the Earth, learning to harness their energies for healing, protection, and transformation. You've been equipped with rituals, meditations, spells, and a multitude of magickal methods, from art magick and culinary magick, to movement and sigil spells, plant magick, charm bags, and more. All of these methods and all of this knowledge has been geared toward empowering your activism, strengthening your connection with the natural world, and aiding in your personal and collective fight against the pressing issues of our time.

But the journey doesn't end here. Closing this book shouldn't signal an end, but rather a new beginning—a call to action. Now, more than ever, the world needs solarpunk witches. We need individuals who are willing to dream of a brighter, greener future, and who are brave enough to do the work necessary to bring that future to fruition. It's time for us to take our knowledge, tools, and insights and use them to light the path toward the sustainable, equitable future we envision.

Your solarpunk witchcraft journey may start with small, individual actions—casting spells to foster global positive change, celebrating Esbats and Sabbats in a way that respects our natural world, or using your magickal practice to uplift your community. But remember, each step you take is part of a much larger movement. You are part of a vibrant, resilient web of solarpunk witches, activists, environmentalists, organizers, and social justice warriors, each working in their own way to sow seeds of positive change.

Never forget the potent power you hold as a witch and as a steward of this Earth. Every spell you cast, every ritual you perform, every intention you set contributes to the world's healing. You are a beacon of hope, a vessel of transformation, and a crucial part of the solarpunk vision.

As you step forward from this book and back into your life, carry with you the energy of the Sun and the resilience of the Earth. Remember the lessons learned and the spells cast. Embrace the radical hope that solarpunk instills. Let your magick and your activism weave together to create a powerful force for change. In every action, in every word, be a solarpunk witch.

The world is waiting for your light.

Let it shine.

Appendix: Recommended Resources

WITCHCRAFT CRAFT RESOURCES

- *The Spiral Dance: A Rebirth of the Ancient Religion of the Goddess* by Starhawk
- *Wicca: A Guide for the Solitary Practitioner* by Scott Cunningham
- *A Practical Guide for Witches: Spells, Rituals, and Magic for an Enchanted Life* by Ylva Mara Radziszewski
- *The Crooked Path: An Introduction to Traditional Witchcraft* by Kelden and Gemma Gary
- *Buckland's Complete Book of Witchcraft* by Raymond Buckland
- *Everyday Sun Magic: Spells & Rituals for Radiant Living* by Dorothy Morrison
- *Drawing Down the Sun: Reclaiming the Magic of the Solar Goddesses* by Stephanie Woodfield
- *Moon Magic: Your Complete Guide to Harnessing the Mystical Energy of the Moon* by Diane Ahlquist
- Llewellyn's Annual Sabbats Almanac
- *Sabbats: A Witch's Approach to Living the Old Ways* by Edain McCoy
- *Llewellyn's Complete Book of Correspondences: A Comprehensive & Cross-Referenced Resource for Pagans & Wiccans* by Sandra Kynes
- *Cunningham's Encyclopedia of Magical Herbs* by Scott Cunningham
- *Magical Herbalism: The Secret Craft of the Wise* by Scott Cunningham
- *A Witch's Guide to Spellcraft* by Althaea Sebastiani
- *Green Witchcraft: A Practical Guide to Discovering the Magic of Plants, Herbs, Crystals, and Beyond* by Paige Vanderbeck

- *Moon Spells: How to Use the Phases of the Moon to Get What You Want* by Diane Ahlquist
- *Bayou Whispers: Ancient Secrets and Spells of the Swamp* by Lana Moon
- *Spell Jars for Beginners: The Modern Witch Compendium with 56 Magic Recipes to Manifest All Your Desires* by Alyssa Vera
- *Kitchen Witchery: Unlocking the Magick in Everyday Ingredients* by Laurel Woodward
- *The Book of Candle Magic: Candle Spell Secrets to Change Your Life* by Madame Pamita
- *Crystal Witchcraft for Beginners: A 5-Step Guide to Cast Spells, Harness the Power of Healing Stones and Crystals for Witches to Unlock the Mind, Chakras, Energy Protection, and Emotional Healing* by Estelle A. Harper
- *Scrying for Beginners* by Donald Tyson
- *Llewellyn's Complete Book of Divination: Your Definitive Source for Learning Predictive & Prophetic Techniques* by Richard Webster
- *Earth, Air, Fire & Water: More Techniques of Natural Magic* by Scott Cunningham
- *Water Magic (Elements of Witchcraft, Book 1)* by Lilith Dorsey
- *Air Magic (Elements of Witchcraft, Book 2)* by Astrea Taylor
- *Fire Magic (Elements of Witchcraft, Book 3)* by Josephine Winter
- *Earth Magic (Elements of Witchcraft, Book 4)* by Dodie Graham McKay

SOLARPUNK RESOURCES
- *Solarpunk Magazine* (SolarpunkMagazine.com)
- Andrewism, a solarpunk YouTube channel
- "Solarpunk: An Introduction" by Sam Paul, FeministBookClub.com

- "Solarpunk: A Reference Guide" by Jay Springett, Solarpunks. net/Ref
- "Solarpunk: A Container for More Fertile Futures" by Jay Springett, SolarpunkMagazine.com
- "Building Utopia Pt 1: Utopia in the Age of Climate Crisis" by Justine Norton-Kertson, SolarpunkMagazine.com
- "Building Utopia Pt 2: How to Tell if the Future You're Building is Utopian" by Justine Norton-Kertson, SolarpunkMagazine.com
- "Building Utopia Part 3: Harmony Between Humanity, Technology, and Nature" by Justine Norton-Kertson, SolarpunkMagazine.com
- "Solarpunk and Technology: A Necessary Relationship?" by Justine Norton-Kertson, SolarpunkMagazine.com
- "Respecting Animal Sentience is a Key Step Toward Building Utopia" by Justine Norton-Kertson, SolarpunkMagazine. com
- "What Sets Solarpunk Apart? Alternative vs Possible Futures" by Justine Norton-Kertson, SolarpunkMagazine. com
- "Putting the Punk in Solarpunk" by Justine Norton-Kertson, SolarpunkMagazine.com
- *Almanac for the Anthropocene: A Compendium of Solarpunk Futures*, edited by Phoebe Wagner and Brontë Christopher Wieland
- World Weaver Press (WordWeaverPress.com)
- Android Press (Android-Press.com)

LUNARPUNK RESOURCES
- "What is Lunarpunk?" at SolarpunkDruid.com
- "The Lure of Lunarpunk" by Kenneth Silber, SpliceToday. com

- "The Nonbinary Nature of Solarpunk/Lunarpunk" by BrightFlame, SolarpunkStation.com
- "Lunarpunk, in hindsight . . . or foresight" by BrightFlame, BrightFlame.com
- "Lunarpunk," Aesthetics.Fandom.com (Aesthetics Wiki)
- "What is Lunarpunk?" by Justine Norton-Kertson, SolarpunkMagazine.com
- "The Matrix Resurrection Brings Lunarpunk to the Big Screen" by Justine Norton-Kertson, SolarpunkMagazine. com
- *Bioluminescent: A Lunarpunk Anthology*, edited by Justine Norton-Kertson
- "What is Lunarpunk, And Can It Fix Solarpunk's Problems?" by Isaac Payne, SignalsFromTheEdge.org

CLIMATE CHANGE RESOURCES

- U.S. Department of Interior's Internet Resources on Climate Change: DOI.gov/library/internet/climate#Data
- Climate Watch (ClimateWatchData.org)
- The Climate Institute, Climate.org
- Climate Action Network International (ClimateNetwork. org)
- Union of Concerned Scientists (UCSUSA.org/climate)
- "Resilience in the Age of Climate" by Art Works for Change (Google Arts & Culture)
- "36 Organizations Helping Solve the Climate Crisis" by Allison Reser, FoodTank.com
- Organizing for Environmental Justice: The Center for Popular Democracy (PopularDemocracy.org)
- National Oceanic and Atmospheric Administration (Climate. gov)
- Climate Science & Policy Watch, Whistleblower.org

- "The Economics of Climate Change" by Sir Nicholas Stern, Head of the U.K. Government Economic Service and Advisor to the Government on the Economics of Climate Change and Development
- *An Inconvenient Truth: The Planetary Emergency of Global Warming and What We Can Do About It* by Al Gore
- *Encyclopedia of Global Warming &Climate Change* by George Philander

SOCIAL JUSTICE RESOURCES

Antiracism

- *The New Jim Crow: Mass Incarceration in the Age of Colorblindness* by Michelle Alexander
- *How to Be an Antiracist* by Ibram X. Kendi
- *So You Want to Talk About Race* by Ijeoma Oluo
- *The Antiracist: How to Start the Conversation about Race and Take Action* by Kondwani Fidel
- *Fascism Today: What It Is and How to End It* by Shane Burley
- *Systemic Racism 101: A Visual History of the Impact of Racism in America* by Living Cities with Aminah Pilgrim, PhD
- *The 1619 Project*, created by Nikole Hannah-Jones
- *White Fragility: Why It's So Hard for White People to Talk About Racism* by Dr. Robin DiAngelo

Trans and Nonbinary Rights

- *Beyond the Gender Binary* by Avlok Vaid-Menon
- *Transgender Warriors: Making History from Joan of Arc to Dennis Rodman* by Leslie Feinberg
- *Gender Outlaws: The Next Generation* by Kate Bornstein and S. Bear Bergman
- *Gender Euphoria*, edited by Laura Kate Dale

- PFLAG's Transgender Reading List for Adults: PFLAG. org/resource/transgender-reading-list-for-adults/
- New York Public Library's List of Transgender Reads
  - For Adults: NYPL.org/books-more/recommendations/ trans-reads/adults
  - For Teens: NYPL.org/books-more/recommendations/ trans-reads/teens
- "13 Books to Better Understand Trans and Nonbinary Lives, Recommended by Activists and Authors" by Hannah Holway, *The Strategist UK*

Disability

- *Disability Visibility: First-Person Stories from the Twenty-First Century*, edited by Alice Wong
- The Disability Justice Resource Center (DisabilityJustice. org)
- *Care Work: Dreaming Disability Justice* by Leah Lakshmi Piepzna-Samarasinha

General Social Justice

- *Making Space for Justice: Social Movements, Collective Imagination, and Political Hope* by Michele Moody-Adams
- *Race and Social Justice: Building an Inclusive College through Awareness, Advocacy, and Action*, edited by Kendra Jason, PhD
- *Our Enemies in Blue: Police and Power in America* by Kristian Williams

About the Author

O nce upon a time, Justine Norton-Kertson corrupted young minds by teaching high school history, civics, and economics from a leftist perspective. Without tenure, finding jobs was tough, so they shifted and spent almost a decade as a union organizer. Nowadays, Justine continues working to corrupt the youth, primarily as a publisher, author, screenwriter, and podcaster. Justine was named one of the 2023 Grist 50 Fixers for their work publishing climate fiction and organizing around climate change, including founding and organizing the annual Utopia Awards & Climate Fiction Conference. She started Android Press and *Solarpunk Magazine* in 2022 and is editor-in-chief for both. Her short stories and poems have been published by *Utopia Science Fiction Magazine, Reckoning, Solarpunk Magazine*, and World Weaver Press, among others. Justine is also the creator and host of the Star Trek fandom podcast *Unimatrix Zero* and the fantasy fiction podcast *Imagitopia* and is an associate producer for the podcast *The 7th Rule*. They live in rural Oregon with her partner, puppies, cats, goats, and bunnies, where they enjoy gardening, kayaking, writing, and making short films. They can be found online on Instagram and TikTok @utopianwitchcraft, or at www.justinenortonkertson.com.

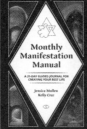

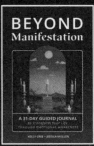

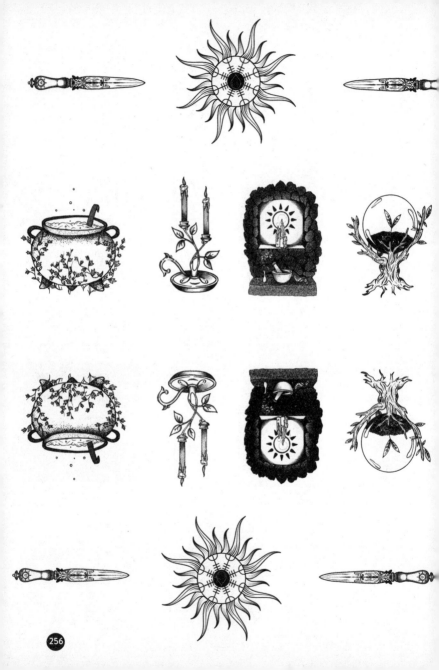